R.E.B.E.L.
FAITH

(Real, Empowered, Bold, Encouraged and Living in the Word)

30-Day Devotional

REBELFAITH

NERISSA E. GRIGSBY

Concise Publishing
Copyright © 2020 by Nerissa E. Grigsby

ISBN: 978-1-7359906-0-6

Book Cover Design by Britton Holmes
Interior Design by Madison Lux

To My Family

Dad, Rev. Victor J. Grigsby; Mom, Vickie; siblings: Tareka, Nekesha, Victor, Alonna, Brian and Clarissa and my nieces and nephews—you all have inspired me and supported every single endeavor and idea that I desired to accomplish! You all helped push and encourage me to accomplish all of my dreams! I love you more than words can express!

To The Readers

My prayer is that as you read each devotional, it will encourage, strengthen, and challenge you to be all that God has destined you to be! Be a rebel faith walker for Jesus!

CONTENTS

Preface vii

Day 1:　R.E.B.E.L. Faith 1

Day 2:　Change Requires A Challenge. 5

Day 3:　Check Your Bags. 9

Day 4:　Don't Panic, but **P.I.V.O.T.** 13

Day 5:　R.E.S.E.T.—Reflect, Exhale, Surrender,
　　　　　Evoke and Treasure! 17

Day 6:　Get a **C.L.U.E.**—Consistently Living Under
　　　　　Evaluation. 23

Day 7:　**D.O.U.B.T.**—Don't Own Unnecessary
　　　　　Baggage Today 27

Day 8:　The Ripple Effect. 33

Day 9:　The **E.N.D.**—Entirely New Direction 37

Day 10:　Underdog 43

Day 11:　You're Not A Failure .47

Day 12:　Increase My Faith 51

Day 13:　Letting Go 55

Day 14:　**D.E.L.A.Y.**—Denying Elevation Looking At
　　　　　Yesterday. 59

Day 15:　Detox 65

Day 16:　Climbing Higher. 71

Day 17:　The Masquerade 77

Day 18:　Indescribable 81

Day 19: Living In Overflow 85
Day 20: Momentum. 91
Day 21: **D.R.E.A.M.** 97
Day 22: **CLAP**back 103
Day 23: Trust When You Can't Trace. 109
Day 24: Get Out Your Feelings 115
Day 25: Divine Assurance 119
Day 26: Get Out of Your Own Way. 123
Day 27: **B.L.I.N.D.**—**B**ound **L**ooking **I**n **N**arrow
Directions 129
Day 28: It's On The Way 135
Day 29: Triumph 141
Day 30: New Season. 147
About The Author 153

PREFACE

This devotional is for anyone! Whether you enjoy reading a devotional as your morning routine—spending time in God's presence before getting ready for the day; or if you are going through some hard times and you need a daily boost of encouragement to remind you not to give up and to keep going! Maybe you need to be challenged in your comfort zone, or you simply need a reminder that God is still with you and there is greater in store for your life! Whatever category you fall in, this devotional is for you! This devotional is meant to be a personal conversation between you and I. I provide personal stories to engage with you, along with spiritual examples and how the topic for the day can be applied.

Now, why would I call a Christian Devotional "**R.E.B.E.L. Faith**?" Well, you will hear more about that by simply starting with Day 1, but as a believer in Christ, I am certain we are all called to be rebels in some way, shape, or form! Jesus was a rebel who went against the grain and did not conform to society or what was deemed "proper protocol." Jesus was a leader and became *"...all things to all men,"* that He might win/save them. (**1 Corinthians 9:19-23 KJV** for context) We are called to do the same and be Rebel Faith Walkers for God! **Romans 12:2 KJV** says, *"And be not conformed to this world: but be ye transformed by the renewing of your mind, that ye may prove what is that good, and acceptable, and perfect, will of God."*

Hebrews 11:1 KJV says, *"Now faith is the substance of things hoped for, the evidence of things not seen."* Our faith in Christ causes us to stand out and be rebels—to stand for, stand on and believe in His promises! Because of this, **R.E.B.E.L.** is an acronym: **R**eal, **E**mpowered, **B**old, **E**ncouraged and **L**iving in the Word. We need to be **real** about what we face day-to-day; **empowered** to beat the odds and fight for our dreams; be **bold** in Christ and not afraid to take a stand; be **encouraged** to keep trying, to never give up and not be defeated; while **living** in the Word, which will grant you life and that more abundantly! (**John 10:10**)

Each day you read the devotional, there will be a closing prayer and a "journaling/notes" section for you to jot down your thoughts. **NOW MEN** … don't go thinking that "journaling" is just for women. Really use that section and take time to seek the Lord and notate what He is telling you to do, change, or implement! The "journaling/notes" section will pose questions and sentence starters such as:

- What I took away from today's devotional is…
- I realize I still struggle and will work on…
- I will cast out these negative thoughts, fears and insecurities today…
- I will speak these positive affirmations over myself today…

Finally, each "journaling/notes" section will end with an affirmation that says, "I will have a good day and it will be better than yesterday! In Jesus Name, Amen!" This is not just an affirmation, but a declaration because you have the authority to speak to your day and proclaim positivity to whatever may come ahead!

This 30-day devotional is meant to encourage you through good times, challenge you where you are comfortable, and speak life to you, in order for you to achieve all that God has ordained for your life! I pray that God speaks to you through these pages! As you read the stories and scriptures, may your life be encouraged, strengthened, and challenged to be all that God has destined you to be!

I Pray God's Richest Blessings Upon You, Nerissa

DAY 1

R.E.B.E.L. Faith

*"To the weak I became weak, so that I might win
the weak. I have become all things to all people,
that I might by all means save some."*

1 Corinthians 9:22 NRSV

When we think of *"rebel"* it's not perceived to be positive. The very definition is one of conflict. In the dictionary, rebel is defined as one who rises in opposition or armed resistance against an established government or ruler. Rebellion is the act or process of resisting authority, control or convention. Rebel has a negative connotation and is definitely not something that most Christians would associate with; or should we?

Jesus was a rebel! He went to unlikely places, met with unlikely people and did not follow protocol. Jesus went against the grain from what society, culture and even what the religious people, the Pharisees and Sadducees, said was right and proper. Nothing about Jesus being a rebel is negative. Rebel can be associated with Jesus because He had a divine purpose; it was for the sake of the gospel—to save people and point them to the Father! The writer of **1 Corinthians 9:22-23 NIV** says, *"To the weak I became weak, to win the weak. I have become all things to all people so that by all possible means I might save some. I do all this for the sake of the gospel, that I may share in its blessings."* If

1

Jesus can be associated with doing things outside of the box, then we need to do the same and be rebel faith walkers for Jesus!

Can we be **r**eal, **e**mpowered, **b**old, **e**ncouraged and **l**ive in the Word **(R.E.B.E.L.)** while having faith in what we don't see and have yet to see come to pass? **Hebrews 11:1 KJV** says, "*Now faith is the substance of things hoped for, the evidence of things not seen.*" As believers in Christ we should step out on faith and go against the grain. The late Honorable John Lewis once said, "Get in good trouble, necessary trouble." Jesus got into good trouble so why don't you? Be like Jesus!

> If Jesus can be associated with doing things outside of the box, then we need to do the same.

So, what can you do? For you, maybe that means mentoring a young person who needs a positive role model. Take the initiative to get the help you need and seek counseling today. Start working on what you're passionate about. Share your gifts and talents with the world. Share your testimony with someone because your story is meant to be heard and it has power to help someone else! There are so many things that we can to do today to become rebel faith walkers for Jesus!

So, are you a REBEL? Activate your **Rebel Faith** today!

God, thank you for being a rebel and not conforming to the pattern of this world. I pray that you give me the strength to be a rebel like you were and increase my faith to be all that you have called me to be. Allow today to be the day I start walking in my purpose and be a rebel faith walker for you! In Jesus name, Amen.

What I Took From Today's Devotional Is:

_____

_____

_____

_____

I Realize I Still Struggle and Will Work On:

_____

_____

_____

_____

I Will Cast Out These Negative Thoughts, Fears, and Insecurities Today:

_____

_____

_____

_____

I Will Speak These Positive Affirmations Over Myself Today:

_____

_____

_____

_____

I will have a good day and it will be better than yesterday!
In Jesus Name, Amen!

DAY 2

Change Requires A Challenge

"The Lord Himself goes before you and will be with you; he will never leave you nor forsake you."
Deuteronomy 31:8 NIV

M ost of us, if we are honest, don't like change. We want to remain comfortable. Too much movement causes us to feel disturbed and disruption is unsettling. It gets us off our game. It causes us to second guess our moves. Disruption causes us to feel unstable. Repetition on the other hand, gives us a sense of normalcy, ensuring that we can keep going with our daily activities. With this routine, we know what to expect. There's nothing wrong with that to a certain extent. Yes, we should all feel a sense of accomplishment and it does feel good to know that what we do on a day-to-day basis is not in vain. We deserve to feel valued and feel like what we do is not taken for granted. It's not wrong to have a sense of pride in our work and feel successful. We should have some order and structure to our day, but what happens when our routines of life and constant repetition is not moving us beyond where we are?

I constantly hear from people that they want to achieve more, that there has to be more to life

To get "more" requires you to get out of your comfort zone and step out into the unknown.

than what they are doing. To get "more" requires you to get out of your comfort zone and step out into the unknown. The uncharted waters of life will flow us into new streams of possibility! Stepping into the unknown requires change and change will be challenging! We don't like the unrest. We don't like the unknown. We don't like the unfamiliar. Human beings have an innate need for security and to have a sense of control and stability. Change will inevitably disrupt that, but it will be worth it!

Where God wants to take you and what He wants to do in your life will require change! This change is different for everyone. Maybe you desire to hear from God in a new way, to hear His voice like never before. In order to do that, the Lord is calling you to spend more time with Him, but it will require you to get up early, consecrate, fast and pray. **It's a challenge!** Maybe you desire to live a long life and not take as much prescribed medication anymore that the doctor has prescribed. In order to do that, the Lord is saying you need to change your eating habits, stick to a healthy diet and an exercise regime.

Whatever change the Lord is calling you to will require sacrifices!

It will require commitment, consistency and discipline. **It's a challenge!** Maybe you desire to be in a healthy relationship, to be loved by someone who will value and support you. The Lord may be saying I have someone for you, but you need to allow me to heal your heart and be open to the process. **It's a challenge!** Maybe it's stepping out and starting your own business. Maybe it's restoring a broken relationship. Maybe it's accepting your call into ministry. Maybe it's writing your first book. Maybe it's launching into a new career that gives you a better sense of purpose and gives you more time with your family. Whatever change the Lord is calling you to will require sacrifices! You may even have to face your fears. Whatever your change is today, it may be difficult, but the Lord is with you! The writer of **Deuteronomy 31:8 NIV** says, *"The Lord Himself goes before you and will be with you; He will never leave you nor forsake you."*

This week, ask yourself what you want to accomplish. What are your dreams? Spend time with the Lord and seek His guidance. Don't be afraid to step out of your comfort zone into uncharted waters because that is where new possibilities lie! Change requires challenge!

Lord, thank you for affirming that you are always with me, even when I can't feel you near! You will never leave me nor forsake me. Give me the strength, the endurance, and the patience to step out of my comfort zone to do what you have called me to do! Help me, Lord, to step out on faith and to trust you. Help me and guide me in Jesus name, Amen!

What I Took From Today's Devotional Is:

_____

_____

_____

_____

I Realize I Still Struggle and Will Work On:

_____

_____

_____

_____

I Will Cast Out These Negative Thoughts, Fears, and Insecurities Today:

_____

_____

_____

_____

I Will Speak These Positive Affirmations Over Myself Today:

_____

_____

_____

_____

I will have a good day and it will be better than yesterday!
In Jesus Name, Amen!

DAY 3

Check Your Bags

"Therefore, since we are surrounded by so great a cloud of witnesses, let us also lay aside every weight and the sin that clings so closely, and let us run with perseverance the race that is set before us.

Hebrews 12:1 NRSV

I am sure that many of you are music lovers! Personally, I enjoy jazz, pop and of course, gospel. I also like rap and trap music, but my favorite is R&B! I especially love R&B music from "back in the day" including: Earth Wind and Fire, Frankie Beverly and Maze, the Whispers and the Temptations—all legends whose music will never die. I can listen to Bilal, Joe, Jill Scott and my all-time favorite, Anita Baker all day long! Another iconic and extremely eclectic artist is the phenom, Erykah Badu. I admire her creativity and authenticity. She has a song titled, *"Bag Lady."* Do you remember that? Some of the lyrics are, *"Bag lady you gone hurt your back, carryin all them bags like that. I guess nobody ever told you—what you hold on it- is you, is you, is you. One day he gone say you crowded my space, one day he gone say you crowded my space...."*

I thought about *"Bag Lady"* and how it actually has a significant testimony and lesson that we all (not just women) can learn from. We carry too many bags. We have bags for days.

We have baggage from our past like dealing with resentfulness, bitterness and unforgiveness. We have baggage from climbing the corporate ladder and being workaholics. We have baggage from trying to exceed everyone's expectations, let alone our own expectations of ourselves. And some of us actually have shopping bags—we try to buy our way into happiness; we try to fill voids that money can't buy.

We all have bags—insecurity bags, low self-esteem bags, financial bags, bad habit bags—and we try to smoke and drink our problems away thus leaving us with addiction bags, complacency bags, bags of tradition, health bags and even children bags, and those problems end up giving you bags under eyes LOL My point is that we all have bags, but like Eryah Badu said, *"You gone hurt yourself carryin all them bags like that. What you hold on it—is you, is you, is you."* Get out of your own way! You're crowding your space. You're crowding the Lord's space! The writer of **Hebrews 12:1 NIV** says, *"Therefore, since we are surrounded by such a great cloud of witnesses, let us throw off everything that hinders (strip off every weight that slows us down— **NLT**) and the sin that so easily entangles us (the sin that easily trips us up—**NLT**). And let us run with perseverance (endurance) the race marked out for us (set before us—**NLT**)."*

In the Bible there are countless individuals who had to check their bags. David gave up his bags, the armor that King Saul wanted to give him to fight Goliath and instead he used what he knew and trusted in the Lord Almighty. (**1 Samuel 17:38-39**) Ruth gave up her bags and renounced what she knew and was accustomed to and told Naomi *"Where you go I will go; and where you stay I will stay. Your people will be my people and your God will be my God."* (**Ruth 1:16-17 NIV**) Esther let go of her bags and said, *"And if I perish, I perish."* (**Esther 4:16 NIV**) She trusted in God to not only deliver her, but to deliver her people!

The Bible is filled with so many stories of people who had "bags" and took the initiative to check their bags and move forward in what the Lord had destined for them to do!

When you fly on a plane, you have to check your bags before you can get to your destination. You check your bags, go through security, wait a little while and then board. There may even be some carry-ons that have to be put away and stowed before the flight can begin. Take-off can't happen until you check/stow your bags. The Lord wants you to take-off, but your bags are holding you down. Check your bags today—those bags may be weighing you down and putting unnecessary pressure on you. Allow the Lord to launch you into something greater!

The Lord wants you to take-off, but your bags are holding you down.

Check your bags so you can take-off!

Lord, I thank you that you can deliver me from baggage. I'm thankful that you are able to give me the wisdom and strength I need to overcome the weight that slows me down and keeps me from accomplishing that which you have for me. God, I'm asking that you help me with the bags that I have. Help me to check those bags and let go! Help me to get out of my own way! In Jesus name, Amen.

What I Took From Today's Devotional Is:

_____

_____

_____

_____

I Realize I Still Struggle and Will Work On:

_____

_____

_____

_____

I Will Cast Out These Negative Thoughts, Fears, and Insecurities Today:

_____

_____

_____

_____

I Will Speak These Positive Affirmations Over Myself Today:

_____

_____

_____

_____

I will have a good day and it will be better than yesterday!
In Jesus Name, Amen!

DAY 4

Don't Panic, but **P.I.V.O.T.**

"Then the Lord answered me and said: Write the vision; make it plain on tablets, so that a runner may read it. For there is still a vision for the appointed time; it speaks of the end, and does not lie. If it seems to tarry, wait for it; it will surely come, it will not delay."
Habakkuk 2:2-3 NRSV

We are not exempt from the unknown happening. Life happens; life is unpredictable. The unknown hits us and when it does, what is our response? Does the unknown and unpredictability of life cause you anxiety, stress, pain, and feelings of being overwhelmed or frustrated?

When my life took a turn and I found myself in a hole that I couldn't get myself out of, I panicked. The situation caused me so much anxiety and stress because I'm the type of person that has to have a plan. I'm type A so I have to have a plan for EVERYTHING. It has to be organized and if it doesn't work out, then I need to go to my plan B, then C, etc. What I found is that at the root of panic is fear… fear of the unknown, simply just not knowing what's coming or what to expect. Fear of not being good enough or fear that things won't work out. If they don't work out, what

P.I.V.O.T.
Persistence, Insight, Vision, Optimism and Triumph

Don't panic… **P.I.V.O.T!**

do I do? Fear of not meeting other people's expectations of me, let alone the expectations I put on myself. FEAR!

In the book of Genesis, we meet Joseph who was loved by his father and had dreams. But in **Genesis 37**, life happened for him. Joseph's brothers plotted to throw him into a pit and kill him. From there, the brothers decided not to kill him, but sell him into slavery. A downward spiral happens to Joseph from that point on—he's put in jail, gets overlooked and forgotten about, and then is falsely accused, just down right lied on, by Potiphar's wife. Life happened for Joseph! He couldn't predict it and he couldn't get out of it on his own. The Word doesn't tell us Joseph's thoughts or emotions, but I have to believe that Joseph didn't panic. Instead he pivoted. I've coined **P.I.V.O.T.** to mean **p**ersistence, **i**nsight, **v**ision, **o**ptimism and **t**riumph. Joseph is in a pit, put there by his own flesh and blood, yet if you read the rest of the story he gets to the palace!

Don't panic… **P.I.V.O.T**!

P—You must have **persistence**. Persistence to overcome any obstacle in life! Persistence in your thinking, to stop thinking negatively and focus on what you believe. You must be persistent in your actions, to keep going after what you believe wholeheartedly. Keep sending the emails. Keep reaching out. Keep asking and seeking the Lord for guidance. Your persistence will open doors. The writer of **Matthew 7:7-8 NIV** says, *"**Ask** and it will be given to you; **seek** and you will **find**; **knock** and the door will be **opened** to you: For everyone that asks receives; the one who seeks finds; and to the one who knocks, the door will be opened."* Be persistent! Ask, seek, knock and you will find what you need and doors will open for you!

I—You must have **insight**. Even if you can't physically see your way out, your reality doesn't dictate or determine your outcome. Insight will force you to see your world from a different perspective. *"Now faith is the substance of things hoped for, the evidence of things not seen."* **(Hebrews 11:1 KJV)**

V—You must have **vision** to see beyond your current reality and focus on your dreams and ideas. Your vision brings about new possibilities. Vision brings the 'not yet' into the right now! Vision will catapult you to your purpose! *"Write the vision, and make it plain upon tables, that he may run that readeth it."* **(Habakkuk 2:2 KJV)**

O—You must have **optimism** in spite of the bad times and know that things won't always be the way they are. Trouble won't last always. Optimism is belief that you will make it through. *"See, I am doing a new thing! Now it springs up; do you not perceive it? I am making a way in the wilderness and streams in the wasteland."* **(Isaiah 43:19 NIV)**

T—You must have **triumph**. You have to see yourself as successful, as already having accomplished that which you believe will to come to pass. Triumph says that you are victorious, you are a conqueror, you can make it and you have the will to win. View your goal, see yourself at the finish line and walk-in triumph! *"Now thanks be unto God, which always causeth us to triumph in Christ, and maketh manifest the savour of his knowledge by us in every place."* **(2 Corinthians 2:14 KJV)**

We can take a lesson from Joseph. Don't panic, but **P.I.V.O.T**! Be persistent and insightful, have vision and optimism and expect triumph in your life!

God, thank you that you in advance that you give me the strength to pivot! Help me to see things the way you see them. Help me to have better insight and wisdom. God grant me vision to see my experiences from a different lens, with a different perspective. Help me to be more positive during my day! Help me to be more optimistic and help me to live in triumph rather than and not defeat! I have the victory in you. In Jesus name, Amen.

What I Took From Today's Devotional Is:

_____

_____

_____

_____

I Realize I Still Struggle and Will Work On:

_____

_____

_____

_____

I Will Cast Out These Negative Thoughts, Fears, and Insecurities Today:

_____

_____

_____

_____

I Will Speak These Positive Affirmations Over Myself Today:

_____

_____

_____

_____

I will have a good day and it will be better than yesterday!
In Jesus Name, Amen!

DAY 5

R.E.S.E.T.—Reflect, Exhale, Surrender, Evoke and Treasure!

"The Lord is my light and my salvation; whom shall I fear? The Lord is the strength of my life; of whom shall I be afraid."

Psalm 27:1 KJV

I am not an electronic expert. I would say that I have a love/hate relationship with electronics. I know enough to get me by, but I am definitely not a guru by any means. I have a lot of different devices. One thing I have found out though with these products is that when they glitch and mess up, it requires a reset. Sometimes it's by simply turning the device off and waiting a few minutes before turning it back on, but in other instances it requires a hard reset. Sometimes, a hard reset is needed to delete cache or cookies from the device and to clear the backend so it will operate the way it was intended. In order to do this, I **Reflect, Exhale,** have to hold two different buttons down **Surrender, Evoke** at the same time and then wait for it to **and Treasure!** power off. I wait a little bit, then restart the device. I recently had to do this with a device, and it got me thinking—at what point do we, as believers, take a reset? We are constantly running, day in and day out, but when do we reset to get recharged so we can clear out the debris and operate the way God has intended us to?

R.E.S.E.T.—I use this word not only for the true meaning, which is to set, adjust or fix in a new or different way, but also as an acronym: **R**eflect, **E**xhale, **S**urrender, **E**voke and **T**reasure!

Reflect—Take time to slow down today and reflect on your life—where you are, what you have accomplished, what you want to accomplish, the journey you are on right now, all that you have been through and the many things to come. We have gotten so busy with our daily routines, that we rarely take time to stop and reflect. Take time to reflect on life itself—God's creation, feel the wind blow, allow the sun's warmth to sweep over your skin, listen to the birds' chirp, and watch the clouds in the sky. Take time to stop and reflect on life and God's creation and all that He has made. Reflect on the fact that you are still alive, reading this devotional right now. Taking time to stop and reflect will not only de-stress you, but will let you have a greater appreciation for all that God has created and what He is still doing in your life.

Exhale—Take a deep breath in and exhale! As you breathe out, breathe out everything that is negative. Every negative thought, every negative feeling, every negative emotion. We need an exhale. With everything going on in our lives and the world today, we need an exhale. Drown out the negative and release that which is toxic and damaging to your soul. You are a spiritual being having a physical, human encounter and we need to allow our spirit to take over. Exhaling will re-center and recalibrate you. Exhaling will allow you to have clarity of thought, mind and spirit so that you can make decisions and not be overtaken or overwhelmed by life's chaos. Take a deep breath in and exhale!

Surrender—One of my favorite songs is *I Surrender All*. The lyrics say, "I surrender all. I surrender all. All to thee, my blessed Savior. I surrender all." We need to surrender. We can't control everything. Shoot, if we really think about it, we can't control anything! Yes, we have free will and we make decisions everyday, but at the core of it all, we are not our own. Surrender your life and will to the Lord. I never want to have the Lord bend His will to my good pleasure. Instead I want to fashion and bend my will to His! *"The Lord is my light and my salvation; whom shall I fear? The Lord is the strength of my life; of whom shall I be afraid."* (**Psalm 27:1 KJV**) Surrender your life to the Lord! Everything that you desire, everything that you hope for, everything that is going wrong—Surrender it to the Lord! He is in control and has ALL power! He can do more with "it," whatever your "it" is, than you ever could! Surrender.

Evoke—Yes, evoke! Invoke is to call upon, whereas evoke is *to call forth*! You can invoke a memory of what the Lord has said upon your life and the word that you know He spoke to you! You can evoke or cause to appear that which you wish to see manifest in your life. The Bible says we are to call *"into being things that were not!"* (**Romans 4:17 NIV**) and that *"The tongue has the power of life and death."* (**Proverbs 18:21 NIV**) You must speak that which you want to see manifest in your life. Speak positivity, healing, restoration and favor. Speak connections, networks and open doors. Speak your RESET as you evoke the Word of God over your life!

Treasure—I look at treasure two-fold. Treasure is great wealth, what we hold dear, what is valuable that we cherish and keep carefully! We need to first make the Lord our treasure! The Bible says, *"For where your treasure is, there your heart will be also."* (**Matthew 6:21 NIV**) What leads you? What are you motivated by? What are you passionate about? We can tell by what's in your heart. Where your treasure is, there the desires of your heart will be. Make the conscious effort to put the Lord back in His rightful place as your treasure! Let Him consume you! Let Him become your heart's desire! Secondly, treasure is not only what we value and keep carefully, but our treasure should also be gratitude for what we cherish! Be grateful! Are we constantly complaining and not taking time to see the true treasures around us? Are we so busy complaining about what we don't have that we miss the treasure right in front of our eyes! Treasure every moment, treasure every memory, treasure our gifts and talents, treasure the grace and mercy that is given to us each and every morning (**Lamentations 3:22-23**) and treasure the time we have! Tomorrow is not promised, so choose to treasure the Lord in your heart and be grateful today!

Is it time that you reset? Do it today! **RESET**—**R**eflect, **E**xhale, **S**urrender, **E**voke and **T**reasure!

God, thank you for the challenge and the reminder to reset! Help me to rest and be present in you! Help me to take time to get in your presence and hear from you today. Help me to make time for you Lord, and to reflect, exhale and surrender my will to yours. Lord, help me not to take things for granted—those things that I overlook every morning: waking up, being of sound mind, having some ounce of strength, having water, food, clothes, and a roof over my head. God, it may not be what I want, but I do have everything that I need. Lord help me to be more grateful and to not complain but to offer more gratitude for the things I do have. God, I thank you that I evoke and call forth your Spirit to guide me today, to be with me throughout the day, to protect and to cover me. In Jesus name, Amen.

What I Took From Today's Devotional Is:

_____

_____

_____

_____

I Realize I Still Struggle and Will Work On:

_____

_____

_____

_____

I Will Cast Out These Negative Thoughts, Fears, and Insecurities Today:

_____

_____

_____

_____

I Will Speak These Positive Affirmations Over Myself Today:

_____

_____

_____

_____

I will have a good day and it will be better than yesterday!
In Jesus Name, Amen!

DAY 6

Get a **C.L.U.E.**—**C**onsistently **L**iving **U**nder **E**valuation

"Indeed, the word of God is living and active, sharper
than any two-edged sword, piercing until it divides
soul from spirit, joints and marrow; it is able to
judge the thoughts and intentions of the heart."
Hebrews 4:12 NRSV

Growing up, we played the board game 'Clue.' It was a detective game where you had to try and figure out who killed who, where the crime took place, and with what weapon. It was interesting drawing the cards, thinking you knew who the culprit was in your mind and then in one second, your assumption was challenged. You find out you were wrong and had to start over. Gathering the pieces of evidence and trying to figure out who committed the crime was the mission of the game.

> In reading the Word of God, we should allow the Word in return to read us!

I find it interesting that scrutiny we used in the game isn't used (if so, very rarely) when applying the Word of God to our lives. We were always taught in church to pray and read our word, but in reading the Word of God, we should allow the

Word in return to read us! The writer of **Hebrews 4:12 NIV** says, *"For the word of God is alive and active. Sharper than any double-edged sword, it penetrates even dividing soul and spirit, joint and marrow; it judges the thoughts and attitudes of the heart."* The Word of God is living and active. The word can create and it can also discern and judge. There is no part of our life that is beyond the knowing observation of God. The Word of God serves as the eyes of God, seeing everything the heart devises and feels.

Let's get a clue! Let's **C**onsistently **L**ive **U**nder **E**valuation. Now what do I mean by that? Allow the Bible to read you— your innermost thoughts, your mood, your attitude, your soul, mind, will, emotions, spirit and body! The Word of God can probe, penetrate and reveal! Allow the Word to do a critical evaluation of you as you would when playing a game like 'Clue.' We need to live under the microscope of the Word of God to be challenged and directed. Without this evaluation being done on a daily basis, we will become stagnant.

The Word says, *"You have searched me, Lord, and you know me. You know when I sit and when I rise; you perceive my thoughts from afar. You discern my going out and my lying down; you are familiar with all my ways."* (**Psalms 139:1-3 NIV**) It also says, *"And be not conformed to this world: but be ye transformed by the renewing of your mind…"* (**Romans 12:2 KJV**) Lastly, *"One thing that I have desired of the Lord, that will I seek after; that I may dwell in the house of the Lord all the days of my life, to behold the beauty of the Lord and to enquire in His temple."* (**Psalm 27:4 KJV**)

Seek to **C**onsistently **L**ive **U**nder **E**valuation of the Word of God!

So, get a **C.L.U.E.** today! Seek to **C**onsistently **L**ive **U**nder **E**valuation of the Word of God!

Lord, thank you for the challenge and the reminder that I need to get a clue. Help me to read your Word today and allow it to penetrate my spirit today. Help me with my attitude and emotional displacement issues. Help me to be a better doer of your word and not just a hearer or reader only. Lord, I am asking that you open your Word to me, so that when I read it, it will also be reading me! In Jesus name, Amen.

What I Took From Today's Devotional Is:

_____

_____

_____

_____

I Realize I Still Struggle and Will Work On:

_____

_____

_____

_____

I Will Cast Out These Negative Thoughts, Fears, and Insecurities Today:

_____

_____

_____

_____

I Will Speak These Positive Affirmations Over Myself Today:

_____

_____

_____

_____

I will have a good day and it will be better than yesterday!
In Jesus Name, Amen!

DAY 7

D.O.U.B.T.—Don't Own Unnecessary Baggage Today

"Jesus said to him, 'Have you believed because you have seen me? Blessed are those who have not seen and yet have come to believe."

John 20:29 NRSV

Doubt! It hits us in different ways. Some may question whether they are good enough—good enough for the job, good enough for the position, good enough to lead, or good enough for the promotion. Some question if they are ready—ready to be married, ready to be in that relationship, to be independent; to go to the next level, or start the business. Others question if they can handle it—asking, "Can I handle the added responsibility? The pressure? The weight? The time commitment and requirements? Some may even question if they can do it—"Can I start the business when it failed the first two times? Can I make ends meet if I step out on faith? Can I get the degree? And lastly, some still question if they will be able to—"Will I be able to live after this divorce? Will I heal from this broken heart? Will I love again? Will I be successful? Will I be able to make next months' bills? Will I be able to have joy again?

Am I good enough? Am I ready? Can I handle this? Can I do this? Will I be able to? These questions and so many more constantly storm our minds and invade our thoughts at any given moment. Life happens! To be honest, all this is baggage that keeps us from going the next mile. It keeps us from stepping out and trying!

D.O.U.B.T.—Don't Own Unnecessary Baggage Today!

At the root of these questions and baggage is a question of belief in your ability to be able to pursue, live up to, achieve and/or simply be! I bought a shirt from a vendor at a church event and the shirt said, "Doubt Your Doubt!" To believe, you have to do just that—doubt your doubt! Doubt the negativity! Doubt the fear! Doubt the frustration! Doubt people's expectations! Doubt your **D.O.U.B.T.—Don't Own Unnecessary Baggage Today!**

Doubt is what Thomas had in the Bible. In **John 20:24-29**, "Doubting Thomas" as he is famously known *(but we will get to this true definition in just a moment)* had an issue. He heard that Jesus resurrected and was alive after being crucified, but Thomas wasn't taking just anybody's word for it. He not only needed to see, but he needed to feel the marks and scars in Jesus' hands and side in order to believe what the other disciples told him.

That is the same for some of us today. Some of us are living in a space where we can't go another step unless we get confirmation (3 times), a prophetic word or dream to accompany it, and reassurance—just anything to reaffirm God's direction. If we don't get the specific signs that we are asking for presented the exact way we want them to be, then we don't move. If we don't hear Him speak, move, or provide extra validation, then we feel a sense of inadequacy. We question what we should do, where we should go, how we should move... and that is all well and good. We *should* seek the Lord's guidance and want that affirmation! The problem comes when we live in a state of complacency and are stagnant because of our own doubt. Doubt breeds low self-esteem, low self-worth, lack of passion and drive, and lack of ambition. Doubt keeps us from even trying to see what is possible! Just try. Like the old adage says, "If at first you don't succeed try, try again."

But... there are some principles that we can learn from Thomas that will encourage us and keep us moving forward in our walk with the Lord!

1.) You are not alone! You're not the first person to feel the way you feel. You are not by yourself. No, you're not crazy. You're not losing it. You are not the only one. Thomas gets a bad rap because he was verbal and adamant about his need to see Jesus' marks, but he did nothing different than what the disciples did earlier in the same chapter. The disciples' announcement to Thomas is the same one that Mary Magdalene made to them earlier in the text (verse 18). The disciples did not seem to believe Mary Magdalene either. It is only when Jesus appeared to the disciples that evening and He showed them the marks in His hands and side that they realized He was the Lord and they rejoiced (verse 19-20). Thomas just wasn't there at that time. They made Thomas feel bad and inadequate for being a "doubter" when they did the exact same thing earlier. Funny how someone else can call you out, but can't see where they were just delivered from themselves—but I digress!

2.) Your doubt will open the door for God's revelation in your life! Jesus made an appointment to show up and for whom? Thomas! That's right. Jesus made a visit to see Thomas. The doubt you have will open up a door to enable God to move on your behalf! God will come to see about you! In whatever situation you are in right now, God will reveal Himself to you, move on your behalf, make ways, open doors, shut doors, open windows, shut windows, lock and put padlocks on entrances and exits—whatever is needed to get your attention! God will meet you where you are to get you to see Him for yourself!

3.) It's all meant to build your faith! Earlier, I stated I would get to the true definition of "doubting" Thomas. The word "doubt" that is referenced in this text, in the Greek, is translated *apistos*, meaning "unbelieving" and then *pistos* meaning "believing." The Lord wants to transition us from unbelief to belief in our lives. The Lord will not only meet you where you are, He won't leave you there either!

He will give you what you need so that you can be strengthened in your faith. God can use your doubt in a season to build you up and strengthen you along the journey. God wants you to go from unbelief to belief!

> Seeing Jesus is not a prerequisite for believing and having faith in Jesus!

Lastly, verse 29 has always been viewed as a means to bash "doubting/unbelieving Thomas," but it's not actually meant for him. I believe it is meant for future generations of believers. It is a reminder for future generations that *seeing* Jesus is not a prerequisite for believing and having faith in Jesus! You don't have to physically see Jesus to know that He is there, alive, well and active in your life! That verse is for us today!

So, the next time doubt creeps in and you begin to question your belief in yourself, your ability to do, to achieve, to succeed, to pursue—realize that the Lord is trying to strengthen and build your faith in Him! Know that *"Everything is possible for one who believes."* (**Mark 9:23 NIV**)

D.O.U.B.T.—**D**on't **O**wn **U**nnecessary **B**aggage **T**oday!

God, thank you for convicting me and showing me where I have doubt. Thank you for revealing to me that I am not alone in my doubt, but that you are with me, helping me to believe bigger than where I am. Thank you for strengthening my faith to believe in you and in your word! Thank you for not giving up on me and not leaving me where I am. You want to move me to greater things that are in store. Help me to remove 'I can't' from my vocabulary and replace it with 'I can,' knowing with you God, all things are possible if I just believe! In Jesus name, Amen.

What I Took From Today's Devotional Is:

_____

_____

_____

_____

I Realize I Still Struggle and Will Work On:

_____

_____

_____

_____

I Will Cast Out These Negative Thoughts, Fears, and Insecurities Today:

_____

_____

_____

_____

I Will Speak These Positive Affirmations Over Myself Today:

_____

_____

_____

_____

I will have a good day and it will be better than yesterday!
In Jesus Name, Amen!

DAY 8

The Ripple Effect

*"So, whether you eat or drink, or whatever you
do, do everything for the glory of God."*

1 Corinthians 10:31 NRSV

G rowing up, we went to the park often—playing on the
playground, going up and down the slides, the jungle
gym, and swinging on the swings. We would also walk along
the hiking trails that were in the park and those trails would
lead to a small pond or lake nearby. When we came to a pond
or lake, we would pick up rocks along the edge of the water and
skip the rocks. To skip the rock, you had to find a small, smooth
rock (preferably flat). Then you would arch your wrist and flick
the rock just right to see how many "skips" the rock could do
across the water. Ultimately, all of this was to see who amongst
my siblings and my dad could make the biggest ripple. If the
rock would skip 3-4 times, the ripple
effect would be bigger in the water. I **Each one of us has**
use this example to illustrate the fun we **a gift to be used.**
had, but also to show how something
as simple as flicking a rock can cause a ripple effect that grows.

Every single one of us has a gift, a calling, a purpose which
brings us joy. This gift is our "rock" to use to cause a ripple
effect or chain of events to happen in this world. Everything

we do ought to be done to the glory of God! The writer of **1 Corinthians 10:31 NIV** says, *"So whether you eat or drink or whatever you do, do it all for the glory of God."* Each one of us has a gift to be used and when we do that as if unto the Lord, it will not only please the Lord, but it will bring pleasure to our souls and to other people.

What is the ripple effect that you are meant to bring into this world? What impact are you meant to have on those around you? I admonish you to think about the ripple you want to make and what "rock" you will use to skip just right on the waters of life's journey!

In **1 Corinthians 15:58 NIV** it is written, *"Therefore, my dear brothers and sisters, stand firm. Let nothing move you. Always give yourselves fully to the work of the Lord, because you know that your labor in the Lord is not in vain."* Make up in your mind this week to give yourself fully to the work of the Lord. Discover your gift and what impact you can and will make in this world. Do what you know how to do. Do what works best for you! Grind, work, and you will succeed because your labor in the Lord is not in vain!

Make a ripple effect today!

Lord, help me to know what my rock is that you've given me to have an impact in this world. Help me if I feel like the gifts and talents I have aren't significant enough. Help me when I compare my talents and gifts to others and feel mediocre. Help me to see that the gift and talent I have cannot be compared and scrutinized. Allow me this day to accept all that I am and what you have given me and to walk in boldness to express and share those gifts and talents. Help me to walk in my gifting today and always. In Jesus name, Amen.

What I Took From Today's Devotional Is:

_____

_____

_____

_____

I Realize I Still Struggle and Will Work On:

_____

_____

_____

_____

I Will Cast Out These Negative Thoughts, Fears, and Insecurities Today:

_____

_____

_____

_____

I Will Speak These Positive Affirmations Over Myself Today:

_____

_____

_____

_____

I will have a good day and it will be better than yesterday!
In Jesus Name, Amen!

DAY 9

The **E.N.D.**—Entirely New Direction

*"...Eye has not seen, nor ear heard, Nor have
entered into the heart of man The things which
God has prepared for those who love Him."*

1 Corinthians 2:9 NKJV

One of my favorite books is *"Believe Bigger: Discover the Path to Your Life Purpose"* by Marshawn Evans Daniels. In this book, Marshawn provides very practical steps to discover your God-given calling and divine purpose, to do and become all that God has destined for your life. Discovering your purpose may come during very turbulent times; when things aren't going as you planned and life has just thrown the biggest curve ball to interrupt all of your hopes and dreams. Marshawn provides a little glimpse into her life and how God intervened with unexpected circumstances. Those situations moved her from being heartbroken and complacent, to living a transformed and fulfilled life!

Life can knock us down to the point where we want to give up and throw in the towel! Unfulfilled dreams, stagnant realities, complacency, hurt, disappointment, rejection and so many others seem to be our demise, but this is not the end! No, it's not the end! It's really just the beginning! Marshawn says that the **E.N.D.** is an **Entirely New Direction**! We have to make up in our minds daily, sometimes hour by hour, that we are ending what seemed like a dead end and we are going to go in an entirely new direction!

The writer of **Romans 4:16-22 NRSV** says, *"For this reason it depends on faith, in order that the promise may rest on grace and be guaranteed to all his descendants, not only to the adherents of the law but also to those who share the faith of Abraham (for he is the father of all of us, as it is written, "I have made you the father of many nations")—in the presence of the God in whom he believed,* ***who gives life to the dead and calls into existence the things that do not exist***. *Hoping against hope, he believed that he would become "the father of many nations," according to what was said, "So numerous shall your descendants be." He did not weaken in faith when he considered his own body, which was already as good as dead (for he was about a hundred years old), or when he considered the barrenness of Sarah's womb. No distrust made him waver concerning the promise of God, but he grew strong in his faith as he gave glory to God,* ***being fully convinced that God was able to do what he had promised****. Therefore, his faith "was reckoned to him as righteousness."*

We have the power to form what we say!

As the Word of God says, *"It depends on faith."* We have to speak what we desire to see! **Our present reality is governed by the things we say!** *"The tongue has the power of life and death..."* (**Proverbs 18:21 NIV**) We have the power to form what we say! We can build up or tear down! We can destroy or we can plant something new to sprout forth! We can speak life or we can speak death!

It's the **E.N.D.** and start going in an **E**ntirely **N**ew **D**irection!

We can encourage someone or we can talk about them and put them down! The choice is yours!

Make up in your mind today and the rest of this week to say it's the **E.N.D.** and start going in an **E**ntirely **N**ew **D**irection! Say it's the **E.N.D.** and start writing your book. Say it's the **E.N.D.** and start taking an online class to learn a new skill. Say it's the **E.N.D.** and start a new hobby; something that brings you joy each day. Say it's the **E.N.D.** and apply for that new job and start a new career! Say it's the **E.N.D.** to bad habits that only cause you more pain and destruction. Say it's the **E.N.D.** of digging a deeper hole for yourself and make the change you need; start saving, start on your retirement plan, start working out, start a new diet. Say it's the **E.N.D.** and be a mentor to somebody who needs a positive influence in their life. Say it's the **E.N.D.** and share your story, your testimony with someone because it just may be a delivering word to help someone else in need! Say it's the **E.N.D.** and forgive the past so you can move forward with what God has for you in your future! Say it's the **E.N.D.** and step out on faith and ask God, seek Him with your whole heart and *speak those things as not as though they are*! See, if all you can do is focus on someone else's past, that just shows where you're still living and where the other has moved on from! Your past doesn't define you! In fact, it refines you to be all that God has called you to be! Learn from your mistakes. Say goodbye to yesterday because you can't change the past anyway. Move forward with what God has for you! There's greater over the horizon!

Make a declaration today that your tomorrow will not be like today and your future will be greater than your past! Decree and declare that your next 6 months will be better and necessary changes will be made! Decree and declare that your next year will be better and new doors of opportunity and networks will be available to you! Decree and declare that your next 5 years will be remarkable, so much so that what God has in store will blow your own mind! Decree and declare that you won't even be able to fathom the plans that God has for you, for it is written in **Jeremiah 29:11 NIV**, *"For I know the plans I have for you," declares the Lord, "plans to prosper you and not harm you, plans to give you a hope and a future."* Decree and declare **1 Corinthians 2:9 NIV**, *"What no eye has seen, what no ear has heard, and what no human mind has conceived"—the things God has prepared for those who love him."*

So, thank you Marshawn for telling us to Believe Bigger! And now—will you **E.N.D.** it and start going in an **Entirely New Direction?!** I know I am! How about you?

> *Thank you Lord, for challenging me to go in an entirely new direction! Thank you for not giving up on me. You are using life's circumstances to build up my strength to go in a new direction to go in a new direction. Help me to trust you today and always to not follow my plan and my will, but to follow after you! Help me to speak positively over my life and my family's lives. I will decree and declare signs, miracles, and wonders. In Jesus name, Amen.*

What I Took From Today's Devotional Is:

_____

_____

_____

_____

I Realize I Still Struggle and Will Work On:

_____

_____

_____

_____

I Will Cast Out These Negative Thoughts, Fears, and Insecurities Today:

_____

_____

_____

_____

I Will Speak These Positive Affirmations Over Myself Today:

_____

_____

_____

_____

I will have a good day and it will be better than yesterday!
In Jesus Name, Amen!

DAY 10

Underdog

"No, in all these things we are more than conquerors through Him who loved us."

Romans 8:37 NRSV

An underdog is a person who is <u>expected</u> to lose. They are those individuals who are deemed "losers," those who are considered weak and not expected to succeed or accomplish anything. If we are honest, most of us have felt like the underdog at times. When the odds are stacked against you and it looks like you are backed up against the wall, that's the underdog. I'm sure you've been there—when bills can't be paid because you have more month left than money; when you have to rob Peter to pay Paul to make sure the lights stay on; when you're a single mother or single father doing all you can to raise your kids; when you're a student and you not only have to prove yourself to professors, but also have to find out where tuition money is coming from; when you're working two and three jobs just to try and make ends meet; and the list could go on and on. Alicia Keys has a song titled *"Underdog"* that was released in 2020. The lyrics say, "This goes out to the underdog. Keep on keeping at what you love. You'll find that someday soon enough, you will rise up, rise up." It's not going to be easy, but we can defy the odds.

With that said, there is another way to look at the underdog. I prefer to look at an underdog as having nothing to lose! I've heard it said before that the most dangerous person there is, is one who has nothing to lose. But this "dangerous" perspective can be a positive one. The underdog will keep fighting and stop at nothing until they reach their desired goal or destination. That's the persistence, determination and fortitude of an underdog. This type of underdog doesn't wallow in what isn't, it doesn't stay stagnant and will not remain downcast, disheartened and frustrated. No, this type of underdog cultivates what seems impossible and uses that energy to say I'M-Possible! We are given a fighting chance! The writer of **Romans 8:28 KJV** says, *"And we know that all things work together for good to them that love God, to them who are called according to His purpose."* God will work all things out!

Now, how do I know we have a fighting chance? Because there was someone in the Bible who was counted out and looked like an underdog. David! In **1 Samuel 17**, King Saul and the Israelites were fighting the Philistines. One of the Philistines was a huge giant named Goliath. Out of all of the soldiers and warriors out on the battlefield, it is a small shepherd boy named David who steps up to the plate and wants to take on Goliath. David's confidence in the God he served outweighed his small stature, overruled his youth and overcame his approach. David knew he could not stand by and let a giant defy Almighty God! Long story short, it is David, with all the odds stacked up against him, who defeats Goliath with just a slingshot and a stone.

Don't view your circumstances with what you don't have.

Another one of my favorite books is *David and Goliath: Underdogs, Misfits and the Art of Battling Giants* by Malcolm

Gladwell. He talks about the advantages of disadvantages and the disadvantages of advantages. Everything you think is an advantage may actually be a disadvantage and vice versa. Gladwell says that the very thing that gave the giant his size, is the very thing that was also the source of his greatest weakness! The same goes for David. His size, age, and method/choice of weapon seemed to be a disadvantage, but served to be the greatest advantage he had, which destroyed the enemy!

If you are an underdog or have felt like an underdog before, it's all about your perspective! Don't view your circumstances with what you don't have. See what you do have and who's with you because that will be just enough to get you through! The writer of **Romans 8:37 NIV** says, *"No, in all these things we are more than conquerors through Him who loved us."*

Lord, thank you for letting me see a different side of the underdog! I ask that you help me today to see what I may think is a disadvantage and show me the advantages! Help me to see where my strengths are! Help me to use what I have and what you have given me to be the best me I can be! Lord, thank you for your guidance and your wisdom today to allow me to keep going and know I still have a fighting chance. In Jesus name, Amen.

What I Took From Today's Devotional Is:

_____

_____

_____

_____

I Realize I Still Struggle and Will Work On:

_____

_____

_____

_____

I Will Cast Out These Negative Thoughts, Fears, and Insecurities Today:

_____

_____

_____

_____

I Will Speak These Positive Affirmations Over Myself Today:

_____

_____

_____

_____

I will have a good day and it will be better than yesterday!
In Jesus Name, Amen!

DAY 11

You're Not A Failure

"For though they fall seven times, they will rise again."
Proverbs 24:16 NRSV

You're not a failure! Let me repeat it again in case you didn't get it. Let it sink in—**YOU ARE NOT A FAILURE!** We can sometimes beat ourselves up for the decisions we made and wrong choices, but that doesn't make us a failure. You may have taken an L, but you are not a failure! It's through the L's, through loss, that God will show you what He has in store. You're not a failure. You have just tried 10,000 ways that don't work! Yes, you should learn from your mistakes and evaluate and take responsibility for what went wrong and what happened, but that doesn't make you a failure. Bad choices, bad decisions and wrong turns are all a part of life! Many people, and if you're not one of them you know someone, live in regret! There are so many who live in regret, resentment, bitterness and unforgiveness simply because of a bad decision!

The Lord wants to free you today from your sense of failure! You did what you knew to do at the time. You followed your gut, but it didn't work out. Your instinct was wrong. Your thoughts and emotions clouded your judgment. You made a decision

You're not a failure. You have just tried 10,000 ways that don't work!

and you dug yourself into a hole. You chose a deal and it went south and you lost everything. You got into that relationship and it left you drained. You followed your own plan. You did what you thought was best in the moment. You wanted to live and **Failure is not fatal!** experience life, so you said yes to everything. You simply wanted to live and "didn't care." You did what you felt was right at the time. Life is about choices and yes, those choices can have positive or negative consequences, but that doesn't make you a failure. Now, repeating the same cycles, doing the same things over and over and over again while expecting different results—that's just insanity. Failure is not fatal! You are not a failure if the decision you made set you back. So, say it again until you believe it—I AM NOT A FAILURE!

The good news is, God promises that He will restore you! *"And we know that in all things God works for the good of those who love him, who have been called according to His purpose."* (**Romans 8:28 NIV**) *"...I will never leave you or forsake you."* (**Hebrews 13:5 NRSV**) *"Being confident of this, that He who began a good work in you will carry it on to completion until the day of Christ Jesus."* (**Philippians 1:6 NIV**) *"For I am convinced that neither death nor life, nor angels nor demons, neither the present nor the future, nor any powers, neither height nor depth, nor anything else in all creation, will be able to separate us from the love of God that is in Jesus Christ Jesus our Lord."* (**Romans 8:38-39 NIV**)

There are so many examples of how God continues to work things out when we make bad decisions. The infamous prodigal son in **Luke 15** demanded his inheritance before his time, then squandered it on "wild living." It wasn't until he found himself in a pigpen that he came to his senses and went back to his father. There's also King David, in **2 Samuel** who sleeps with Bathsheba and ends up getting her pregnant. As soon as he finds out, he orchestrates a plan to kill her husband Uriah on the frontline in battle. Despite all he did, God never left David. God stayed with him!

It may not be good while it's working, but it will work out for your good! I love the song by Donnie McClurkin titled, *We Fall Down*. It says, "We fall down, but we get up. For a saint is just a sinner who fell down and got up! Get back up again!" God is full of mercy and full of grace. There's no condemnation, just get back up again! *"For a just man falleth seven times, and riseth up again..."* **(Proverbs 24:16 KJV)** No matter what you've done, it's not too late to get back up again! Another scripture I love is **Joel 2:25 NIV**. The word says, *"I will **repay** you for the years the locusts have eaten."* God keeps His promises and His word is true! He will repay, give back, restore and make up for what you thought you lost. So, no you are not a failure today! It may not have worked out the way you wanted it to work out, but God has other plans!

Lord, thank you for affirming that I am not a failure!
Help me to forgive myself. Help me to seek you first in all
of my decisions. Help me to be patient and not move when
I want to move, but when you would have me to move.
Lord, you are a very present help in the time of trouble,
and I need you today and always. In Jesus name, Amen.

What I Took From Today's Devotional Is:

I Realize I Still Struggle and Will Work On:

_____

_____

_____

_____

I Will Cast Out These Negative Thoughts, Fears, and Insecurities Today:

_____

_____

_____

_____

I Will Speak These Positive Affirmations Over Myself Today:

_____

_____

_____

_____

I will have a good day and it will be better than yesterday!
In Jesus Name, Amen!

DAY 12

Increase My Faith

"...Because of your little faith. For truly I tell you, if you have faith the size of a mustard seed, you will say to this mountain, 'Move from here to there,' and it will move; and nothing will be impossible for you."
Matthew 17:20 NRSV

Gospel singer, Brian Courtney Wilson, has a song entitled *Increase My Faith*. I love the lyrics which say, *"To be honest sometimes I wonder if it's come time to pack it in. If I've given my best and there's nothing left so my best days are at an end. Then I remember that you would never let me face what's next alone. I know that you're keeping me, strength when I'm weak and expect me to carry on. I know that the Lord is preparing me for great things I have yet to see, but on days when it's hard to believe increase my faith."* That's what we all need sometimes—an increase of faith when it's hard to believe. When things just don't seem to go right, increase my faith, Lord. When the unexpected happens, increase my faith.

The writer of **Luke 17:5 NRSV** says, *"...Lord, increase our faith."* To provide context, throughout this chapter Jesus is providing instruction and admonishing them to live with a kingdom mindset. He gives them a word of caution, for them to be on guard so they won't stumble. He also encourages them to repeatedly forgive those who sin. The disciples respond to Jesus' elevated standards and their sense of inadequacy in the face of such a high standard, and ask that the Lord "increase their faith!" The disciples' plea conveys the recognition that faith is two-fold. On the one hand, faith is a dynamic process and one can grow in faith. On the other hand, the disciples ask that the Lord add to or strengthen their faith. They recognize that faith is not just a matter of their own strength, but they need the Lord to be able to do this.

> **Faith we have should grow and increase as we commit ourselves to the Lord and trust in Him to make up the difference.**

Their faith fell short with their lack of trust in God's power. Complete trust in God and His power is required to equip you with courage and strength to carry out the Christian mission. It is written in **Matthew 17:20 NIV**, *"...Because you have so little faith. Truly I tell you, if you have faith as small as a mustard seed, you can say to this mountain, 'Move from here to there,' and it will move. Nothing will be impossible for you."* The faith we have should grow and increase as we commit ourselves to the Lord and trust in Him to make up the difference. So, where do you struggle with your faith? Ask the Lord to increase your faith!

God, I ask that you help increase my faith today! Lord, help me to seek after you and live to a higher standard. Lord, I pray that you take my faith from a mustard seed and grow it. Increase the areas where I am weak and help me to trust you with every area of my life. Thank you Lord for strengthening me and increasing my faith. In Jesus name, Amen.

What I Took From Today's Devotional Is:

_____

_____

_____

_____

I Realize I Still Struggle and Will Work On:

_____

_____

_____

_____

I Will Cast Out These Negative Thoughts, Fears, and Insecurities Today:

_____

_____

_____

_____

I Will Speak These Positive Affirmations Over Myself Today:

_____

_____

_____

_____

I will have a good day and it will be better than yesterday!
In Jesus Name, Amen!

DAY 13

Letting Go

"Forget the former things; do not dwell on the past. See, I am doing a new thing, now it springs up, do you not perceive it? I am making a way in the wilderness and streams in the wasteland."

Isaiah 43:18-19 NIV

I've come to discover that you will never move farther than what you hold on to. What do I mean by that? Well I'm sure I'm not the only one, but when I go back home, I see some of the same people sitting on the same corners, wearing their old high school varsity jackets, reminiscing about the "good ole days." Don't get me wrong—reminiscing isn't wrong and is good to do, but the problem is when you stay there. Living there and not moving beyond the 'good ole days' is the problem. You have to let go to move forward. Living in the past and not doing something to plan and prepare for your future. We shouldn't just talk about the past, but we should also talk about the future and what we envision and see for ourselves that is to come.

How do we get stuck in the past? Maybe circumstances have happened in your life and you can't move past the hurt—the hurt of the divorce, the money you lost, the business that went bad, or the friendship that ended. Letting go can be hard because of the pain—the pain

Let go so you can move forward!

of heartbreak, the pain of mistakes, the pain of friends walking away, the pain of disappointment. We have to let go! Let go of your own agenda! Let go of people's expectations. Let go of the lies. Let go of people's opinions. Let go so you can move forward!

If we are honest, letting go can feel like we are losing hope. Your mind may start to wander and conjure up thoughts about what you've lost and how things will never get better. We need to allow the Lord to help us move past the pain and disappointment. The writer of **Isaiah 43:18-19 NIV** says, *"Forget the former things; do not dwell on the past. See, I am doing a new thing! Now it springs up; do you not perceive it? I am making a way in the wilderness and streams in the wasteland."* It is written in **Philippians 3:13-14 NIV**, *"Brothers and sisters, I do not consider myself yet to have taken hold of it. But one thing I do: Forgetting what is behind and straining toward what is ahead, I press on toward the goal to win the prize for which God has called me heavenward in Christ Jesus."* DeWayne Wood said it best in his song titled, *"Let go and let God!"*

Sometimes, the pain we have is too hard to move past— especially the pain and anguish that results from the death of a loved one. Grief and bereavement can stifle our progress. Losing someone is hard to endure and it is NEVER easy to *"move on."* The individual that comes to mind when I think about this is Naomi. In the book of Ruth, Naomi experienced the loss of her husband and her two sons. Interestingly enough, it is Ruth her daughter-in-law, that affirms that Naomi's home, people, God, and tomb will be hers. She says in **Ruth 1:16-17 NIV**, *"...Where you go I will go, and where you stay I will stay. Your people will be my people and your God my God. Where you die I will die, and there I will be buried..."* The word then continues

There are hidden treasures that are revealed in darkness!

by saying Ruth works in the barley harvest, cutting grain in the fields and meets Boaz. Ruth runs home to Naomi and tells her of how she met Boaz and it's through Naomi's wise counseling that helps the situation come to a desired end. God then uses Boaz as an instrument for the resolution of the calamity Naomi and Ruth are facing! Despite the pain Naomi endured, she had someone who would never leave her side. God then used that one person to be a blessing and restore blessings unto her.

Jesus is that one for us who will never leave our side. No matter how bad things get, we have God to rest on. There's an old hymn that says, "Just ask the Savior to help you. Comfort, strengthen and keep you. He is willing to aid you. He will carry you through!"

So, what does this mean for you today? Don't be bitter, resentful or upset over what was taken or what you lost. Why? Because God provides gifts and blessings during times of loss. There are hidden treasures that are revealed in darkness! Healing is a process! We have to trust God in the process to bring us through all the pain and sorrow that we have experienced and endured. The writer of **Romans 8:18 NIV** says, *"I consider that our present sufferings are not worth comparing with the glory that will be revealed in us."* God's glory is being revealed in your life even through the hurt and pain. So, let it go today and let God push you to something new.

Lord, help me to let go. Help me to trust you to let go of the pain that I have experienced. I ask that you restore me, that you remove any bitterness, and remove any resentment and anger from my life. Thank you Lord for the reminder that you will provide blessings during times of loss. I know that you have hidden treasures in my dark season. Thank you God for confirming that what the enemy meant for evil, you are turning it around for good. God help me to forgive, comfort me, and strengthen me to keep going! In Jesus name, Amen.

What I Took From Today's Devotional Is:

_____

_____

_____

_____

I Realize I Still Struggle and Will Work On:

_____

_____

_____

_____

I Will Cast Out These Negative Thoughts, Fears, and Insecurities Today:

_____

_____

_____

_____

I Will Speak These Positive Affirmations Over Myself Today:

_____

_____

_____

_____

I will have a good day and it will be better than yesterday!
In Jesus Name, Amen!

DAY 14

D.E.L.A.Y.—Denying Elevation Looking At Yesterday

*"For I know the plans I have for you," declares
the Lord, "plans to prosper you and not to harm
you, plans to give you hope and a future."*
Jeremiah 29:11 NIV

The dictionary defines delay as a period of time by which something is late or postponed. It can also be used as a verb, which means to make someone or something late or slow. How many of us have wasted time thinking about what happened yesterday? I don't know about you, but I have always spent too much time worrying about the *"shoulda coulda wouldas"*—"I should have done this...I could have done that...I would have done that instead." Worrying about yesterday only delays our tomorrow.

When we delay, consuming our time worrying about yesterday, we don't put enough time and energy into our tomorrow. When we delay, we are **D**enying **E**levation **L**ooking **A**t **Y**esterday. We can't go higher, and we can't be all that God has destined for us to become, by consuming ourselves with yesterday. Yes, we should

> Worrying about yesterday only delays our tomorrow.

take some time to evaluate and assess what happened and what went wrong so we can learn from it, but we can't get enamored with yesterday. That analysis should spark a new vision and help us put a plan together to act on next steps. If we consume our minds and our time with what did or didn't happen yesterday, we won't be able to see the new possibilities that await in tomorrow! Denzel Washington once said, "No one remembers the strike outs, they only remember the homeruns." There's no need to be embarrassed or upset with yesterday. We just have to make up in our minds to be better and do better tomorrow! God has so much in store for us. If we focus on what lies ahead, there is greater in store! The writer of **Jeremiah 29:11 NIV** says, *"For I know the plans I have for you," declares the Lord, "plans to prosper you and not to harm you, plans to give you hope and a future."*

When I think of **D.E.L.A.Y.—D**enying **E**levation **L**ooking **A**t **Y**esterday, I automatically think of the Israelites. In Exodus, Moses told Pharaoh to "Let my people go." After enduring slavery in Egypt, Pharaoh let the Israelites go, but then he chased them. They crossed the Red Sea with Moses' staff in hand, which separated the waters for them to pass through. From there, they were headed toward the promise land—Canaan, but first had to go through the wilderness. Instead of going through the wilderness, they ended up staying in the wilderness, going around in circles for 40 years. The book of Numbers records that while they were in the wilderness they complained. They complained and hated where they were so much that they shifted their mindset back to Egypt. They hated their new environment, the unknown, and the process of their journey. They wanted

> Had you not gone through what you went through, you wouldn't be where you are right now.

to go back. Their mindset was pinned to their time in Egypt and they complained that they should have just stayed where they were.

We may criticize the Israelites, but some of us are just like them. We think about going back to that relationship that was no good and try to justify it by saying, "Everybody has something." We talk ourselves out of not applying for the job because of the credentials and qualifications that we don't think we have, even when we have even more skills and experience than our counterparts. We are constantly filling our minds with thoughts of "I was better off where I was," "I shouldn't have tried this," "What was I thinking," and "I knew this would happen." No one likes delays or detours in life, but delays are just a setup for a comeback! You may need to learn something or experience something while in the delay. Had you not gone through what you went through, you wouldn't be where you are right now, you wouldn't know what you know now, and you wouldn't be who you are! Delays build character. Delays strengthen your faith. Delays make you trust God more!

The infamous church cliché says, "God's delay doesn't mean God's denial." I believe it's not just a cliché, but it is true! When God delays something, it is not God's denial. He could just be setting something else up that is wilder than your wildest dreams! The delay you're in will be worth it and it will be better for you in the end. So, look at your **D.E.L.A.Y.** with a different lens—it's really **D**enying **E**levation **L**ooking **A**t **Y**esterday. Don't prohibit and prolong your elevation. Don't focus on yesterday! God wants to take you higher! Trust Him to work it out in the end!

Lord, thank you for affirming that my delay is not my denial. Help me to realize that I don't need to go backwards. I don't need to dwell on the past and stay in yesterday. You have a plan for me! Lord, help me to trust you. Today please help me to overcome any anxiety or frustration about my yesterday. Lord, help me to live today for a better tomorrow! Pour out your Spirit upon me God and help shift my mindset and perspective. In Jesus name, Amen.

What I Took From Today's Devotional Is:

_____

_____

_____

_____

I Realize I Still Struggle and Will Work On:

_____

_____

_____

_____

I Will Cast Out These Negative Thoughts, Fears, and Insecurities Today:

_____

_____

_____

_____

I Will Speak These Positive Affirmations Over Myself Today:

_____

_____

_____

_____

I will have a good day and it will be better than yesterday!
In Jesus Name, Amen!

DAY 15

Detox

"Do you not know that your bodies are temples of the Holy Spirit, who is in you, whom you have received from God? You are not your own..."

1 Corinthians 6:19 NIV

I'm sure you've heard of detox before. This is a method, not just for weight loss, but also for people who want to cleanse their body of toxins. It can be used to reduce weight, but the goal is to ultimately improve health and rejuvenate the body. When we think about the body, we primarily think about the physical body, but have we ever considered a spiritual detox? Many people when they wake up in the morning, grab their cell phones through the latest updates and stories on social media. Many people turn on the TV to check the news and the weather. Some get up early to attend their favorite workout class or simply try to get in some type of activity before starting the day. Yet others go right to preparing for the day—taking a shower, getting dressed, get the kids ready, making coffee and starting breakfast. For some, the morning is always a rush, constantly running behind so breakfast or working out is not an option.

At what point in our daily routines, whatever that may consist of, do we start with the Lord? Now I know some of you out there are saying, "That is me—I do start every morning praying and thanking God for another day. I read my word, even pick up this devotional and read the day that's planned." (Shameless plug, I know). The point is, does your spirit need something fresh? Is it the constant, same routine over and over? Is your spirit not getting anything new?

You can't grow being stagnant. You can't grow being comfortable.

Have you gotten so accustomed to your routine, whatever it is, that it just comes natural, but it's not feeding you anymore? Your spirit longs for something new. It may be time for a detox.

I can admit that I am not very consistent with a daily routine. I do have a devotional I will read in the morning and will always play worship/praise songs, but I may miss kneeling and praying until midday or even at night. I may miss picking up my Bible until it is time to study for a lesson or prepare to preach. I am at a place where I need to assess my daily routine and do something different to feed my spirit. What things can you do differently? Maybe try meditating—sitting in silence and instead of you talking to the Lord, allow the Lord to talk to you. Maybe sit outside or look out the window and just stare at God's creation and take in all that He has made that we take for granted. Maybe kneel down and thank God for what you do have and not focus on what you don't have. Wherever you are, your spirit wants to be refreshed and rejuvenated. Maybe you need to detox!

The point of the matter is that you can't grow being stagnant. You can't grow being comfortable. If you've never tried meditating, then maybe challenge yourself to sit silently for five minutes and ask God to speak to you—you may be surprised by what you hear. If you have never turned your phone off or taken a break from social media, you might be surprised by the amount of time you have and what you can do when you're not glued to the phone. Maybe simply picking up the Bible to read a scripture before grabbing your phone could serve as being refreshing. Allow the Word of God to be the first thing you read when you wake up and the last thing you read before you go to bed. It will change things! There are so many things you can do. The Lord is requiring a detox today. Yes, we need to be better stewards of our physical bodies and watch what we put into our bodies—less salt, less sugar, less processed foods, etc., but what about our spiritual bodies as well?

The writer of **1 Corinthians 6:19 NIV** says, *"Do you not know that your bodies are temples of the Holy Spirit, who is in you, whom you have received from God? You are not your own."* This passage is about more than sexual immorality, which the Corinthians had a problem with. They felt they should be free to do whatever they wanted with their bodies. I could get into a theological discussion about how scholars deem this to be about the Gnostic view and that a person's body was an inferior deity and was destined for destruction. This meant that the body was not of importance when it came to their spiritual life, but I won't get into that. The point of this scripture is that the Holy Spirit resides in believers. The Holy Spirits resides in such a way that our bodies, our very selves, have been transformed into a "shrine" dedicated to God. The Holy Spirit and thereby constitutes us a temple. To whom one belongs, and who or what dwells in one, are the same.

Does your temple need a detox today? What can you start doing differently today to ensure that not only physical toxins, but spiritual toxins are removed from your body? What can you start doing that will build up your spiritual health and rejuvenate your soul? Think about it—do you need a spiritual detox? Try it. It just might make you not only feel better, but live better too!

God, thank you for your Spirit that dwells on the inside of me. I don't take it for granted and I know that you are with me every day. Lord, help me to be better with my time. Help me to have a spiritual routine that not only detoxes, but also rejuvenates my soul. Help me to see where I can do things differently and try something new. Lord, I want to hear from you today and I want to be cleansed from anything that is not like you. In Jesus name, Amen.

What I Took From Today's Devotional Is:

_____

_____

_____

_____

I Realize I Still Struggle and Will Work On:

_____

_____

_____

_____

I Will Cast Out These Negative Thoughts, Fears, and Insecurities Today:

_____

_____

_____

_____

I Will Speak These Positive Affirmations Over Myself Today:

_____

_____

_____

_____

I will have a good day and it will be better than yesterday!
In Jesus Name, Amen!

DAY 16

Climbing Higher

"Know that I am with you and will keep you wherever you go, and will bring you back to this land; for I will not leave you until I have done what I have promised you."
Genesis 28:15 NRSV

When I was young, I would attend numerous services. I am a PK (preacher's kid) so we had 2 services almost every Sunday; not to mention prayer meeting, bible studies, revivals; you name it—I had to attend. When I would go to my grandparents' church, they had old school devotional service, not praise and worship like we have today. That was when the deacons would get up in front of the church, sing songs and invite others in the congregation to stand up and give a testimony or sing a song before service would start. Without fail, someone would always stand up and give their testimony starting with, "First giving honor to God, who is the head of my life." Then they would end by singing a song called, "Jacob's Ladder." The lyrics are as follows: "We are climbing Jacob's ladder. We are climbing Jacob's ladder. We are climbing Jacob's ladder. We are climbing Jacob's ladder. Soldiers of

> One of the essential keys to success in life is a dream, a vision, something to drive us to greater things.

the cross." There were other verses, but that one always got me when I was little.

I had no clue what the words actually meant back then, but I thought it was fun because it kept repeating and the melody sounded similar to that of nursery rhythm that my dad would sing to us. As a kid, my imagination ran wild, so it was fun to imagine Jacob pulling out a ladder from his garage and inviting everybody to take turns climbing. I didn't know where we were going, or what the destination was, but I thought it was a game to climb up and down the ladder and then give someone else a turn. (I was young ok—don't judge me LOL)

This song was actually a negro spiritual that slaves would sing. This song gave them hope to climb, not physically, but spiritually, to take their mind off of the pain and agony. It let their spirits focus on being free—whether in this life or in Heaven with the Father.

I didn't realize until I got older that "Jacob's Ladder" was about the connection or bridge per say, between Heaven and Earth. The prayers and testimonies that we say in the house of God are the connections straight to God's ears. As you pray and petition the Lord, each level takes you higher. It's an ascension. Just as Christ departed from Earth and ascended into Heaven, we long to ascend one day to be where Jesus is.

Jacob's ladder is taken from **Genesis 28:10-19**. The vision of the ladder, or more accurately a stairway or ramp, is one that comes from a dream. One of the essential keys to success in life is a dream, a vision, something to drive us to greater things. Jacob needed a dream! His possessive mother, Rebekah, had schemed with him

> You can't fix what you're not willing to face!

to take his brother's birthright away, resulting in Esau's wrath. Before Esau could kill him, Jacob ran away. In his running,

Jacob has a dream in Bethel and envisioned God's angels sent from Heaven to Earth on their divinely appointed missions.

So, what does this mean? Maybe you are not physically a slave like our ancestors were when they were singing this song hoping for a better day to come, but maybe you are fleeing from something. Maybe you are on the run from yourself, running from a call on your life, or simply running because it's easier to run than to deal with the present circumstances. Maybe you are hoping for a better day to come! But you can't fix what you're not willing to face! The Lord desires that you climb higher! Climb higher in Him. He desires intimacy—in-to-me-see. God wants you to see into Him. There's a hymn that says, "Have a little talk with Jesus. Tell him all about your struggles. He will hear our faintest cry and He will answer by and by. When you feel a little prayer wheel turning and you know that the fire is burning, just a little talk with Jesus will make it right." Talk to the Lord! Your "ladder" is your bridge or stairway to Heaven! Your ladder is your lifeline to the Savior. Climb higher so that you can see what God would have for you to do.

Helen Keller was once asked what would be worse than being born blind. She responded, "To have sight and no vision." So many of us have sight, but no vision for our lives. We have to climb higher and talk with the Master so that we can see over our present situation. You know you can't see through a forest full of trees. It's only when you rise above, fly overhead that you're able to see what's just over the horizon. The Lord is calling you to climb higher today. Climb higher in your thinking of yourself. Climb higher in your thoughts. Climb higher in your conversations with others. Climb higher with your ambitions. Climber higher with your relationship with God! Climb higher!

Lord, thank you for confirming that I need to climb higher!
God, just like you gave Jacob a vision during his turmoil,
give me a vision that will help me in the state I'm in. Lord,
help me to climb higher and to be closer to you. Help me to
face those things that are weighing me down and causing me
to think little of myself. Lord, I want to climb higher and
I'm asking for your help today. In Jesus name, Amen.

What I Took From Today's Devotional Is:

_____

_____

_____

_____

I Realize I Still Struggle and Will Work On:

_____

_____

_____

_____

I Will Cast Out These Negative Thoughts, Fears, and Insecurities Today:

_____

_____

_____

_____

I Will Speak These Positive Affirmations Over Myself Today:

_____

_____

_____

_____

I will have a good day and it will be better than yesterday!
In Jesus Name, Amen!

DAY 17

The Masquerade

"But ye are a chosen generation, a royal priesthood, a holy nation, a peculiar people; that ye should shew forth the praises of him who hath called you out of darkness into his marvelous light."

1 Peter 2:9 KJV

I like to attend all kinds of parties. I like birthday parties, family cookouts, and even formal parties. I'm the life of the party and I will be the first one on the dance floor ready to line dance as soon as I hear the beat drop! I was invited to a party one time and it was a masquerade ball. It was a formal affair. Everyone dressed up in tuxedos and ball gowns and each person had to have a mask. The mask was meant to disguise the individual's face, covering up any key features that would make them recognizable right away. I not only enjoyed the investigation of trying to find the people I knew and guessing who they were, but I also found pleasure in looking at each of the masks. There were masks that had different color paint and art designs, as well as masks that were decorated with gems, rhinestones, diamonds and feathers.

As I tried to look through the holes of the masks to see if the eyes would give a person away, it dawned on me! A masquerade ball is not the only place masks are worn. We don't go around wearing decorative masks physically, but we wear masks all the time. At work we wear masks when we have to code switch. You know, we put on the professional voice at work to ensure our intelligence is heard. We wear masks around our friends, hiding things that we should talk about and seek help for. Heck, we wear masks on social media, posting only the good pictures (that have been edited with the right filter) to floss and show everyone what an amazing life we have. We even wear masks at church, with the same ole' cliché responses, "I'm blessed and highly favored," when in reality we are hurting on the inside. I have come to discover God can't bless who you pretend to be! It's time to stop the masquerade and drop the masks!

God can't bless who you pretend to be!

As children of the Most High God, we are called to stand out! The writer of **1 Peter 2:9 KJV** says, *"But ye are a chosen generation, a royal priesthood, a holy nation, a peculiar people; that ye should shew forth the praises of Him who hath called you out of darkness into his marvelous light."* The issue for the people of 1 Peter is their status in the eyes of God versus their status in the eyes of the larger world, in which they were despised exiles. In the context of Isaiah, we are reminded that the chosen people are in the wilderness and they are exiles. Yet even in the desert, God shows them to be His own and He cares and provides for them. The phrases "royal priesthood" and "holy nation" are specifically drawn from **Exodus 19:6 KJV**. These verses recall the story of the Israelites' exodus from Egypt. It reminds them once again that God delivered the despised people of Israel from their enemies and after the time of their wandering in the wilderness, brought them to the promise land.

So, what's the point? We can't continue to walk aimlessly through the wilderness, masking areas that the Lord wants to heal. Don't hide behind the mask of life. Maybe it's counseling;

seek the help you need. Forgive the one that hurt you; let go of the weight and move on. Stop pretending; be your authentic self. Don't mask who you are and who God has called you to be to fit in or conform to social pressures. Be who you are! We are a chosen people, a royal priesthood. The writer of **Deuteronomy 14:2 NIV** says, *"For you are a people holy to the Lord your God. Out of all the people on face of the earth, the Lord has chosen you to be his treasured possession."* We were made to stand out, to be rebel faith walkers for Jesus. The Lord will bring you to your promise land! Whatever He has purposed you to do, He will bring it to pass. So, stop the masquerade, take off the mask, and stop hiding. Live your abundant life now!

We can't continue to walk aimlessly through the wilderness, masking areas that the Lord wants to heal.

Lord, thank you for reminding me that I stand out for a reason. You have made me peculiar and I don't need to hide. Help me to stand in who I am and be unapologetically me. Help me to remove the masks that I have used to cover up who I really am. I stand on your Word and believe that you will deliver me. Help me to remove the masks that I have used to cover up certain areas of my life. Help me to trust you to fulfill the promises you have for my life. In Jesus name, Amen.

What I Took From Today's Devotional Is:

_____

_____

_____

_____

I Realize I Still Struggle and Will Work On:

_____

_____

_____

_____

I Will Cast Out These Negative Thoughts, Fears, and Insecurities Today:

_____

_____

_____

_____

I Will Speak These Positive Affirmations Over Myself Today:

_____

_____

_____

_____

I will have a good day and it will be better than yesterday!
In Jesus Name, Amen!

DAY 18

Indescribable

"Delight yourself also in the Lord, and He shall give you the desires of your heart.
Psalm 37:4 NKJV

I love the lyrics of Kierra Sheard's song, "Indescribable." *"Indescribable, uncontainable. You place the stars in the sky and you know them by name. You are amazing God. All powerful, untamable. Awestruck we fall to our knees as we humbly proclaim. You are amazing God. Incomparable, unchangeable. You've seen the depths of my heart and you love me the same. You are amazing God."* God truly is indescribable! No matter how many words we try to piece together to express all that He is, we will always come up short. God is truly indescribable!

We can sometimes lose sight of how amazing God truly is! We can lose sight of God's majesty by being so busy. We tend to forget all that He really is—how God moves on our behalf and shields us from danger seen and unseen, and provides for us. If we are honest, many of us worship God as we want Him to be, not as He truly is! For many of us, God has become our own "genie in the bottle" and if we rub him the right way, we will

If we are honest, many of us worship God as we want Him to be, not as He truly is!

get our wish; But God is not our genie! He is not an entity to be blackmailed or persuaded like, "Okay God if I do this then you do that." It doesn't work that way!

The psalmist says in **Psalm 37:4 KJV**, *"Delight thyself also in the Lord; and He shall give thee the desires of thine heart."* The thing is, if we delight in the Lord, He becomes our desire. When

When you become so consumed with God, your desires become His.

you become so consumed with God, your desires become His. I used to think of this scripture as a simple equation like 1 + 1 = 2; like, if I do something good and seek God, then I can expect something good from God in return or He'll give me what I want. But the idea of

You + God is the majority!

delighting ourselves in God means we make Him the most important thing in our lives! When He is the number one desire of our hearts, He will give all of Himself to us. When we have God, we have all we need. You + God is the majority! God is truly indescribable!

We can become so consumed with life, that we begin to worship other idols and replace God with other things. We can worship our favorite sports team, money, status, power, phones, our own comfort, self, and even our kids. It is written in **Revelation 2:4 NIV**, *"Yet I hold this against you: You have forsaken the love you had at first."* Is God drawing you back to Himself? Is God calling you to worship Him in a different way—wholeheartedly, in Spirit and in truth? The writer of **John 4:24 NIV** says, *"God is spirit, and His worshipers must worship in the Spirit and in truth."* Take a second just to think about if you truly worship God

Survival depends on God's presence.

for who He is? Does God really leave you in awe of His power and glory? Is there an area in your life that needs to be challenged when you think about this? God is truly indescribable!

There is something about being truly in awe and in reverence of God! When I think of this, I think of Moses. **Exodus 33:17-23** is a passage about God's glory. Earlier in the chapter, Moses asked to know God's ways and then he asked to see His glory. When Moses asked to see the glory of God, the Lord showed him His back. God tells Moses, *"No one sees my face and lives."* The primary agenda of this entire chapter revolves around the fact that survival depends on God's presence. Moses didn't stop at his first request, but he kept going and kept asking until He got to see the glory of the Lord. Have we been that persistent before, to just ask to see His glory? I'm talking about not asking God for anything, not demanding that you get something in return, but just adamant about seeing the presence of Almighty God! Our very survival depends on God's presence in our lives! God is truly indescribable!

We should be in awe of our God! We should fill our minds with the revelation of a God who is both mighty and merciful, a God who is both gracious and great! My prayer is that all of us will be stunned with the majesty of God, that we be left breathless in His presence, and amazed by His strength! God is truly indescribable!

> *Lord, help me today to be in awe of you. Help me to get back to you as my first love! God, I will put you back at the top as my priority, to desire you above all else. Help me Lord today to not only make time for you, but experience your presence in a way that I haven't previously. Reveal yourself to me in such a way that I become in awe of your glory, of your presence, of your peace, and of your power! Lord, you truly are indescribable. In Jesus name, Amen.*

What I Took From Today's Devotional Is:

_____

_____

_____

_____

I Realize I Still Struggle and Will Work On:

_____

_____

_____

_____

I Will Cast Out These Negative Thoughts, Fears, and Insecurities Today:

_____

_____

_____

_____

I Will Speak These Positive Affirmations Over Myself Today:

_____

_____

_____

_____

I will have a good day and it will be better than yesterday!
In Jesus Name, Amen!

DAY 19

Living In Overflow

*"But seek first the kingdom of God and His righteousness,
and all these things shall be added to you."*

Matthew 6:33 NKJV

Nothing about God is mediocre. As God's children, our lives are not meant to be mediocre either. Many times, our mediocrity comes because we settle for less than what we **We lack striving to achieve higher because of our own self-limitations.** deserve. We lack striving to achieve higher because of our own self-limitations. We second-guess ourselves! Dr. Cindy Trimm has a book entitled, *Hello Tomorrow* and she says, "We are all grown up, but conditioned by our self-imposed limitations and paradigms of lack, failure, and a just-getting-by mentality; conditioned to always think and act like followers when we are leaders; conditioned to fail when we are innately wired to succeed." She is exactly right! We have our own chains—those self-limiting beliefs that hold us back, whether they're childhood experiences, past failures, or lies we were told that we chose to believe. With those chains we live mediocre lives. God has destined more for you! You can live an abundant life today by starting with what the writer says in **1 Peter 5:7 NIV**, *"Cast all your anxiety on Him because He cares for you."*

Scripture tells us that, *"The thief comes only to steal and kill and destroy; but I have come that they may have life, and have it to the full."* (**John 10:10 NIV**)

Jesus is not selfish like the enemy. The enemy only wants what satisfies itself, but God cares about all of us and desires for us to be close to Him. When we connect and commune with Him, we receive an abundant life of purpose and fulfillment that the world can't give and the world can't take away. When we accept Jesus into our hearts, we receive our identity as members of His flock, a community of believers. By having Jesus as our point of access to God, we receive abundant life! Jesus provides an abundant life, a life to the full—being fulfilled and satisfied in Him.

Your spiritual maturity and growth toward the likeness of Jesus Christ, will always be in proportion to the greatness of the God you know!

In this day and age, when we think of overflow, we tend to assume that it means money or materialistic abundance; an overflow of wealth, an overflow of possessions, or even an overflow of time and days on this Earth. I'm not saying that God won't give you those things, but God's abundant life is to be experienced and lived through Him! To live abundantly God will give you things that money cannot buy—an overflow of peace, love, joy, wisdom, understanding, and patience.

I can recall when I was younger, sitting at my grandparents' kitchen table eating a huge breakfast that was prepared. One thing that was inevitable was my grandfather having a mug sitting on a small saucer and he would pour his coffee. By the time he put in his cream and sugar, the coffee would be to the brim of his mug. When he stirred the contents, the coffee dripped down the side and onto the saucer. When he finished his coffee, he would remove the mug, take the saucer in his hands and then slurp the remaining coffee from the saucer. That's overflow! When you have more than enough and there is still some leftover for you to enjoy, that's overflow. Just when you think it's gone, there is still excess that remains!

Abundant in the Greek is *perisson*, which means all-around excess, more than, beyond what is anticipated, more than one can expect, exceedingly or beyond measure. There is more than you can ever expect when you live through God our Savior. The writer of **Ephesians 3:20 NIV** says, *"Now to Him who is able to do immeasurably more than all we ask or imagine."* It is written in **Matthew 6:33 KJV**, *"But seek ye first the kingdom of God and His righteousness and all these things shall be added unto you."* If we seek the Lord, everything else will follow.

Do you not know that your spiritual growth is governed by the greatness of the God you know? If you make God small, you will be small. If to you God's power **If you don't know Him, you will immobilize Him in your life!** is limited and confined, so will your power. Your spiritual maturity and growth toward the likeness of Jesus Christ, will always be in proportion to the greatness of the God you know! But if you don't know Him, you will immobilize Him in your life! You will stagnate and limit God from moving in your life!

You were meant to live a life of abundance, to live in overflow, but you can't enjoy someone you don't know! It starts with getting to know the Master, our Savior, the King of Kings and the Lord of Lords, the Everlasting Father, the Great I Am! Living in overflow comes when you live in Him!

Lord, thank you for reaffirming that I have an abundant life in you! Lord, I'm not going to let my history interfere with my destiny! I'm going to start living my abundant life today! Today is a new day and I am casting all my cares, worries, anxieties and limitations onto you! I cast out those things and ask that you pour into me your wisdom, love, peace, joy and direction. Help me today to not confine or limit your power in my life! Thank you for reminding me today that I have abundance in you. In Jesus name, Amen!

What I Took From Today's Devotional Is:

_____

_____

_____

_____

I Realize I Still Struggle and Will Work On:

_____

_____

_____

_____

I Will Cast Out These Negative Thoughts, Fears, and Insecurities Today:

_____

_____

_____

_____

I Will Speak These Positive Affirmations Over Myself Today:

_____

_____

_____

_____

I will have a good day and it will be better than yesterday!
In Jesus Name, Amen!

DAY 20

Momentum

"I will lift up my eyes to the hills—from where will my help come? My help comes from the Lord, who made heaven and earth."

Psalm 121:1-2 NRSV

I'm one of seven children to my parents and growing-up we always went to amusement parks. My mom's job always gave away tickets to their employees and respective families to attend Kennywood Park. Now, for those not from Pittsburgh, Pennsylvania or familiar with Kennywood, it could be described as a smaller Six Flags or Kings Dominion. It was our place to have fun, let loose and enjoy some rides.

Ok, let me pause and explain something—I HATE heights! I am tremendously afraid of heights; being in the air with no real sense of security. I remember riding a roller coaster when I was young with my dad and uncle and I almost fell out! When it ended, I ran off of the roller coaster with tears in my eyes and vowed I wouldn't ride one again. That trauma, I guess, stuck with me, as I got older.

At Kennywood Park it was guaranteed that my siblings would want to ride all the roller coasters in the park. We would have to wait in line for the longest time and it never failed that when I would get to the front of the line to get in the seats,

everyone would jump in and start locking in their seatbelts...
but not me! There would be a knot in the pit of my stomach and
I just couldn't do it. I would then retreat to the nearest exit and
wait for them to come off and meet me at the walkway to head
back to our parents. Toward the end of the day, I would finally
get sick and tired of them teasing me about not getting on any
of the roller coasters. Even with the knot in the pit of my
stomach and butterflies swarming, I reluctantly would get on.
As the last attendant double-checked the seat belt and harness,
the rollercoaster started to climb.

So, here I was in this roller coaster seat and I couldn't turn
back. As it climbed, I could hear the dreaded clicking sound as
the chains ascended the cart higher and higher on the tracks.
It was beyond nerve racking! Everyone else was laughing and
screaming in amusement and I was crying.
My siblings told me to look at the scenery **The momentum**
and see the view, but I kept my eyes closed. **you need is in**
I was terrified, screaming "Get me off of **the climbing!**
here!" The clicking stopped as the cart
rounded the top curve and dropped us into what seemed like a
never-ending doom to eternity. I kept my eyes closed, hunched
down in my seat and screamed bloody murder until the end.
When it was all over, my siblings and I looked at the camera
footage and I was again the laughingstock of the family for the
day, as my face in the picture was evidence of my horror.

I say all of this, not only to provide you with a funny story
to imagine as you start your day, but to get you to think about
how momentum starts. A roller coaster climbs higher and
higher, with the clicking sound of the chain, ascends to the
highest point and then it takes off. The roller coaster gains
kinetic energy to continue the remaining loops and turns until
the end. Some of you right now are in the climbing phase. It

seems like everything is an uphill battle! It's hard to stay focused because you may be distracted by the *clicking* noises around you. You may be fearful of what's up ahead and how far you have to go up. Know today that the uphill battle is only taking you higher so you can have the momentum to continue the rest of the ride! The momentum you need is in the climbing! Climbing is what builds your strength, your character, your tenacity and your endurance. The climb may be scary, and you may even be afraid, but remember that you had the courage to get on the ride in the first place!

The climb will give you the momentum you need to finish your journey and reach your intended goal!

Don't let anyone stop you or put you down! The ride you are on is taking you to a place you never even thought would be possible. You may have tried it before, but you didn't go all the way. You may have attempted to get on, but you refused to go through with it and walked away. Give yourself some grace and be proud of the fact that you got on for the ride! Now that you're on, the climb will take you where you need to go! The climb will give you the momentum you need to finish your journey and reach your intended goal! The climb won't last forever. It may be hard to take for a while, but the release is coming! The release is coming to take you to your destination.

Look at your climb differently. See it from a different perspective. Scripture says, *"I will lift up mine eyes unto the hills—from whence cometh my help. My help cometh from the Lord, which made heaven and earth."* (**Psalm 121:1-2 KJV**) The imagery in Psalm 121 is a journey. It is a profession of faith in God's protection and providence—the divine care of God, but protection from what? In the Psalm, the mountains/hills seen in the distance bring about caution and hesitation because of fear of falling or stumbling. The mountains/hills describe and single out an elevated terrain that poses a threat of difficulty and potential danger. The mountain has to be climbed in order to get to the other side, to the intended destination, but concern and anxiety begin to set in. The Psalm says to take heart because there is safety from the Father to protect and keep us on the journey! The mountain can be looked at as a potential concern to conquer, but if we change our perspective, we can see the mountain as looking towards Mt. Zion—the holy and eternal city! Our help comes when we turn our perspective from seeing that mountain as a threat, to seeing it as the divine protection that is provided on our journey!

I've heard it said, "The best view comes after the hardest climb!" Your help is on the mountain. Your help is in the climb! So, climb higher, so that your momentum can propel you forward! Your momentum comes from the climb!

Lord, thank you for your Word and letting me know that you are taking me higher to propel me forward! God, help me to not get frustrated and distracted during the climb. Help me to see it from a different lens. Lord, let me have a new perspective about my uphill battles. Lord, I trust you that you are allowing every climb to take me higher so that you can push me forward. Thank you Lord for the momentum. I receive it. In Jesus name, Amen!

What I Took From Today's Devotional Is:

_____

_____

_____

_____

I Realize I Still Struggle and Will Work On:

_____

_____

_____

_____

I Will Cast Out These Negative Thoughts, Fears and Insecurities Today:

_____

_____

_____

_____

I Will Speak These Positive Affirmations Over Myself Today:

_____

_____

_____

_____

I will have a good day and it will be better than yesterday!
In Jesus Name, Amen!

DAY 21

D.R.E.A.M.

*"Commit to the Lord whatever you do,
and He will establish your plans."*

Proverbs 16:3 NIV

The legend and great Civil Rights leader, Dr. Martin Luther King Jr. had a dream. He said, *"Let us not wallow in the valley of despair, I say to you today my friends. And so even though we face the difficulties of today and tomorrow, I still have a dream. It is a dream deeply rooted in the American dream. I have a dream that one day this nation will rise up and live out the true meaning of its creed: "We hold these truths to be self-evident, that all men are created equal."… I have a dream that my four little children will one day live in a nation where they will not be judged by the color of their skin but by the content of their character. I have a dream today! … I have a dream that one day every valley shall be exalted, and every hill and mountain shall be made low, the rough places will be made plain, and the crooked places will be made straight; and the glory of the Lord shall be revealed and all flesh shall see it together."* Sadly, this iconic speech is the only thing many recognize Dr. King for, when in fact he did so much more! He had an economic plan to end poverty and he never got to see his dream fulfilled.

Given the state of today's world and the issues we face, it

doesn't seem like much has changed and we are still fighting for justice, equality and equity for all; especially our African-American brothers and sisters! Despite having a black man as a former President of the United States of America, this country remains dis-united and the dream still has yet to be realized!

No matter what opposition we may face, we should still fight for our dream

But this should not get us down! Even though Dr. King experienced hardships in life, he still pursued his dream and kept going. He didn't let anything stop him! We should take that to heart because no matter what opposition we may face, we should still fight for our dream! The writer of **Isaiah 40:31 KJV** says, *"But they that wait upon the Lord shall renew their strength; they shall mount up with wings as eagles; they shall run, and not be weary; they shall walk, and not faint."* It is written in **Hebrews 12:1-2 NIV**, *"Therefore, since we are surrounded by such a great cloud of witnesses, let us throw off everything that hinders and the sin that so easily entangles. And let us run with perseverance the race marked out for us, fixing our eyes on Jesus,*

Dreams are not just meant to be thought and talked about, but they are meant to be lived!

the pioneer and perfecter of our faith. For the joy set before him he endured the cross, scorning its shame, and sat down at the right hand of the throne of God." It doesn't matter what obstacles you may be facing, what didn't happen before, or what people may think—go after your dreams!

You have a dream and your dream can be a reality! Dreams are not just meant to be thought and talked about, but they are meant to be lived! Your dreams can come to fruition! It's never too late—whether you are seasoned or younger, made many mistakes in your past, or are starting over—your dreams can still be a reality today! The writer of **Hebrews 10:35-36 NIV** says, *"So do not, throw away your confidence; it will be richly rewarded. You need to persevere so that when you have done the will of God, you will receive what he has promised."* You ought to be inspired every day to chase your dreams. It is written in **Proverbs 16:3 NIV**, *"Commit to the Lord whatever you do, and He will establish your plans."* It doesn't matter what your dream is—big or small—go after it with all your heart, mind, and soul!

To pursue your DREAM, you need to:

- **D:** Dare to be different. You were meant to stand out. The writer of **Deuteronomy 14:2 NIV** says, *"For you are a people holy to the Lord your God. Out of all the peoples on the face of the earth, the Lord has chosen you to be his treasured possession."* It is written in **1 Peter 2:9 NIV**, *"But you are a chosen people, a royal priesthood, a holy nation, God's special possessions, that you may declare the praises of him who called you out of darkness into his wonderful light."* Lead and don't be a follower. You weren't meant to blend in, you were meant to stand out.
- **R:** Remind yourself of what the Lord has placed within you. *"For God hath not given us the spirit of fear; but of power, and of love, and of a sound mind."* (**2 Timothy 1:7 KJV**) God has equipped you with everything that you need.
- **E:** Examine where you are and what places, people, and things may need to be removed to get you closer to where you need to be. Let nothing distract you!
- **A:** Affirm your gifts, talents and abilities—even if no one else does! Don't wait on the confirmation or validation from others. You may be waiting a long time!

Believe in yourself and walk in that assurance. God has
you and that's all you need!

- **M:** Manage your time, resources, money, and talents
  wisely. Even if you made mistakes in the past, today
  is a new day to start over. Make strides to implement
  necessary changes to get yourself back on track. Even
  while you're planning and working your plan, be on
  guard. The enemy comes to steal, kill and destroy.
  (**John 10:10**) Stay prayed up and seek advice from wise
  counsel where you need it.

So, what is your dream? Whatever you have been thinking
about—a new career, a new blog, a business, displaying your
talents, starting a family, saving money, investing, retirement, a
new house, rebuilding a relationship, taking on a family project,
moving to a new city—Whatever your dream is, create a vision
board and get started! It can and will happen! The writer of
Habakkuk 2:2-3 KJV says, "*...Write the vision, and make it
plain upon tablets, that he may run that readeth it. For the vision
is yet for an appointed time, but at the end it shall speak and not
lie...*" Start today to make your dreams a reality because your
dreams were meant to be lived!

*Lord, thank you for your Word. Thank you for confirming
that even in the midst of obstacles and opposition, my
dreams are still meant to be lived. Help me to start over
and work on the passions and dreams you have placed on
the inside of me! Help me to stay diligent in the process
when things get hard. Lord, I know you are with me and
I will keep pursuing my dreams. In Jesus name, Amen!*

What I Took From Today's Devotional Is:

_____

_____

_____

_____

I Realize I Still Struggle and Will Work On:

_____

_____

_____

_____

I Will Cast Out These Negative Thoughts, Fears, and Insecurities Today:

_____

_____

_____

_____

I Will Speak These Positive Affirmations Over Myself Today:

_____

_____

_____

_____

I will have a good day and it will be better than yesterday!
In Jesus Name, Amen!

DAY 22

CLAPback

*"But blessed is the one who trusts in the
Lord, whose confidence is in him."*
Jeremiah 17:7 NIV

In today's culture, there are a lot of new terms and sayings. They aren't anything like the old school terms and phrases like: jive turkey, you jivin', can you dig it, right on, get down, catch you on the flip-side, or do me a solid. We went from that, to sayings like: dope, chill/take a chill pill, cool, fly, psyche, out to lunch, cool beans, as if, and boo-ya. Later on, there was slang like: crunk, trippin, homies, whatever, step-off, it's all good, da bomb, phat, roll out, off the chain/off the hook, dawg, bet, and fire. Depending on where you lived, what block you rep'd, who your crew was, what side of town you were from, or even where in the United States you resided (north, south, east, west), your language was different.

Nowadays, we have new terms like: lit, lowkey, salty, slay, shook, shade, periodt, snatched, fit, Gucci, cap/no cap, tea, flex and tried it. There's one in particular that stands out to me and that is the term clapback. You know, it's like a comeback—to respond to something whether an insult or criticism, in a direct manner. A person responds with their comment in what the Urban Dictionary says as, *"Delivering a quick, sharp and effective response, deemed as a targeted, often viciously acute comeback intended to put someone in check."* It's meant to put someone in their place. They came for you, so now you're comin' for them!

I know I am not the only one that has clapped-back on a few people before. Whether I felt I was being wronged, used, mistreated, or taken advantage of, I wanted to justify myself and state my case. As culture says, "Don't come for me 'les I send for you." When I look back on the times that I have done this, I not only wanted to give the person a piece of my mind, but I also wanted to make them feel as bad as they tried or intended to make me feel. I wasn't gonna stand for it and they had the right one! I simply wanted to tell them off so that they knew they could never talk to me like that again! Over time though, I found that it was a divisive plan and trick of the enemy, to allow my mouth to spew out words to only distract me and use me as a pawn to promote more division. Now, don't get me wrong, I'm not saying that you shouldn't stick up for yourself. I believe you shouldn't let people walk all over you. What I am saying is, we get so accustomed to fighting every single battle that we are losing the internal one! We constantly fight everything externally, and in the end, it leaves us drained and stressed out, with blood pressure escalated and headaches. Sometimes, if we would just leave it alone and not say anything at all, the Lord will deal with that situation and person better than we can. We have to use discernment and seek wisdom to know when we should fight, take action, and speak up versus when it's time to put it in the Master's hands.

Think about it as you go to work—dealing with your boss and coworkers; attend school—dealing with your teachers/ professors and classmates; or deal with your family and friends today! Does something have to be said every time? Do you always have to have the last word? Do you always have to put people in their place? Even if they are wrong, is it worth the energy and headache to prove you are right? How much better could your day go if you learned to pick your battles and not fight every single one? How much more energy would you have if you truly decided to cast your cares and burdens on the Lord? Sometimes knowing when <u>not</u> to say something is more important than what you have to say!

Christ vindicates us! We can only receive that vindication when we walk upright and put our trust in Him! It is written in **Psalm 26:1 NIV**, *"Vindicate me, Lord, for I have led a blameless life; I have trusted in the Lord and have not faltered."* The writer of **Deuteronomy 32:36 NIV** says, *"The Lord will vindicate His people and relent concerning his servants when he sees their strength is gone..."* The Lord sees you and has compassion on you! He will give you the strength you need to endure. Give it to God. It is written in **Isaiah 54:17 NRSV**, *"No weapon that is fashioned against you shall prosper, and you shall confute every tongue that rises against you in judgment. This is the heritage of the servants of the Lord and their vindication from me, says the Lord."* The weapon may form, but it won't prosper. Those words may want to form, but know when you need to put them in the Lord's hands! Give it to Jesus.

Currently, a clapback is meant to be derogatory. Today, I want us to see CLAPback in a positive way:

- **C: Confident.** Be confident in your gifts and abilities God has given you. You are who God says you are. Be confident in and through Him. He will help you where you are weak and provide you with strength. Walk in your confidence and trust God to pick up any slack. *"But blessed is the one who trusts in the Lord, whose confidence is in Him."* (**Jeremiah 17:7 NIV**) *"Have I not commanded you? Be strong and courageous. Do not be afraid; do not be discouraged, for the Lord your God will be with you wherever you go."* (**Joshua 1:9 NIV**)

- **L: Loved.** Know that you are loved by God! God loves you and His love is unconditional. Because He loves us, we should love others. *"Beloved, if God so loved us, we ought also to love one another. No man hath seen God at any time. If we love one another, God dwelleth in us, and his love is perfected in us."* (**1 John 4:11-12 KJV**) *"This is my commandment, that ye love one another, as I have loved you. Greater love hath no man than this, that a man lay down his life for his friends."* (**John 15:12-13 KJV**)

- **A: Affirmed.** In Christ we can find validation, emotional support and encouragement. We are affirmed through Christ. Speak affirmations over yourself. Speak positivity instead of negativity. *"My son, attend to my words; incline thine ear unto my sayings. Let them not depart from thine eyes; keep them in the midst of thine heart. For they are life unto those that find them, and health to all their flesh."* (**Proverbs 4:20-22 KJV**)

  No matter what people say or do to you, you are still worth the value that's in you!

  You should also build up one another instead of tear down! *"Therefore encourage one another and build each other up, just as in fact you are doing."* (**1 Thessalonians 5:11 NIV**)

- **P: Priceless.** We are priceless to God. Don't diminish the value that God has placed on the inside of you. *"For we are God's handiwork, created in Christ Jesus to do good works, which God prepared in advance for us to* *do." (***Ephesians 2:10 NIV)** *"As you come to him, the living Stone—rejected by humans but chosen by God and precious to him..."* **(1 Peter 2:4 NIV)**

Here's why you need to CLAPback in this manner. If I had a $20 bill and I asked you if you wanted it, I know you would say yes. If I took that $20 and balled it up in my fist and asked if you still wanted it, you would say yes. If I took that $20 bill and stomped it on the ground then asked if you still wanted the $20, you would still say yes. The point is, no matter what I did to the $20 it was still worth $20. No matter what people say or do to you, you are still worth the value that's in you! No matter what has happened to you, you are still worth the **Walk in a new CLAPback— confident, loved, affirmed and priceless!** value that you were created with! So, make a better effort to watch how you talk and treat people today. Leave the vengeance to the Lord and walk in a new CLAPback—confident, loved, affirmed and priceless!

Lord, I ask that you give me wisdom and discernment today to know when I need to fight, speak up, or take action and when I need to place it in your hands! Lord, I'm asking for your help today. Help me to be a steward of my time, talents and treasures. Help me to watch my mouth and not always feel the need to retaliate every time something happens. God, help me put my trust in you to see me through this day and every day, knowing you are my vindicator. In Jesus name, Amen.

What I Took From Today's Devotional Is:

_____

_____

_____

_____

I Realize I Still Struggle and Will Work On:

_____

_____

_____

_____

I Will Cast Out These Negative Thoughts, Fears, and Insecurities Today:

_____

_____

_____

_____

I Will Speak These Positive Affirmations Over Myself Today:

_____

_____

_____

_____

I will have a good day and it will be better than yesterday!
In Jesus Name, Amen!

DAY 23

Trust When You Can't Trace

"God is our refuge and strength,
a very present help in trouble."
Psalm 46:1 NRSV

Maybe you have been in a place where you know God is real, but you can't seem to trace Him! What is He doing? Why is He being silent? Why won't He do something? What is He up to? Or maybe you are questioning whether God even exists because it's hard for you to see God moving given all the chaos and destruction in the world! We have all experienced questions of theodicy, *the vindication of divine goodness and providence in view of the existence of evil;* the infamous "Why would a loving God allow bad things to happen?" questions of life.

At one point or another in our spiritual journey, especially for those who just started or even those who refuse to believe, we have raised questions like: Is God angry? Is God upset with the world? Is God frustrated with our human activity? Is this the beginning of the end of the world? How could a loving God let such a disaster take place? Is God allowing this to happen? These questions that run through our feeble minds are theological questions of theodicy. We may have many questions and fewer answers, but we can turn to the inspired Word of God! We have to know that God is still our help, He is our fortress, our refuge… God is our strength!

Psalm 46 NRSV says, *"God is our refuge and strength, a very present help in trouble. Therefore, we will not fear, though the earth should change, though the mountains shake in the heart of the sea; though its waters roar and foam, though the mountains tremble with its tumult. Selah. There is a river whose streams make glad the city of God, The holy habitation of the Most High. God is in the midst of the city; it shall not be moved; God will help it when morning dawns. The nations are in an uproar, the kingdoms totter; he utters his voice, the earth melts. The Lord of hosts is with us; the God of Jacob is our refuge. Selah. Come, behold the works of the Lord, see what desolations he has brought on the earth. He makes wars to cease to the end of the earth; he breaks the bow, and shatters the spear; he burns the shields with fire. "Be still, and know that I am God! I am exalted among the nations, I am exalted in the earth." The Lord of hosts is with us; the God of Jacob is our refuge. Selah."*

Psalm 46 was written out of the crucible of extreme adversity from which God had provided deliverance. It relates to anyone who is in trouble, or to anyone who will face trouble, no matter how extreme, in the present or future. It tells us that when trouble comes God is sufficient enough to get us through. No problem we face, whether emotional, physical, mental or spiritual,

> Whatever seems over your head, is under God's feet!

is too big for our God! If we learn to take refuge in Him and lean on Him alone for strength, we can face the most extreme cries with quiet confidence because God is with us and He's more than enough! You + God is the majority! Because He is the God of the universe that holds everything in its place, He also has you in the palm of His hand! That's why you can rejoice because whatever seems over your head, is under God's feet!

Take Job for example. Job suffered and couldn't trace God. He complained and said, *"If I go forward, he is not there; or backward, I cannot perceive Him; on the left he hides, and I cannot behold him; I turn to the right, but I cannot see Him."* (**Job 23:8-9 NRSV**) Job didn't complain because of his suffering. He complained because he couldn't find God while he was experiencing his suffering! Job felt like God was not there. Job couldn't find Him! Yet, in spite of his condition, his loss, his infirmities and his suffering, Job says, *"But he knows the way that I take; when he has tested me, I will come forth as gold. My feet have closely followed his steps; I have kept his way without turning aside. I have not departed from the commands of his lips; I have treasured the words of his mouth more than my daily bread."* (**Job 23:10-12 NIV**) Job trusted God and depended on God's heart, even when he couldn't trace His hand! Job knew it was painful and it didn't make sense, but he still trusted in the God! I believe Job trusted God because even though he couldn't find God, Job knew that God knew where he was!

Job trusted God and depended on God's heart, even when he couldn't trace His hand!

God knows where you are today! Your situation may look bleak, it may seem impossible, but as it's been said… impossible spells I'M-POSSIBLE. Nothing is too hard for God to work out! My pastor, Rev. Dr. Frederick Douglas Haynes III says, *"Only when it's dark enough can you see the stars and on a stormy day with darkened clouds, doesn't negate the existence of the sun!"* It may seem dark right now and you may not be able to trace God's hand, but the SON (not just the sun) is still shining! If you're in a dark place, God is gonna move! You just have to trust Him when you can't trace Him!

Lord, thank you for reaffirming that I need to trust you when I can't trace you! Help me to trust you more today! Lord, I need you to work things out in my life and in my family's lives. Until it comes to pass, help me to continue to seek after you with my whole heart! Lord, I need you to do the impossible in my life. You are my present help in times of trouble. You are my refuge and strength and I will follow your heart, even when I can't trace your hand. I will trust you even when I can't trace you. In Jesus name, Amen!

What I Took From Today's Devotional Is:

_____

_____

_____

_____

I Realize I Still Struggle and Will Work On:

_____

_____

_____

_____

I Will Cast Out These Negative Thoughts, Fears, and Insecurities Today:

_____

_____

_____

_____

I Will Speak These Positive Affirmations Over Myself Today:

_____

_____

_____

_____

I will have a good day and it will be better than yesterday!
In Jesus Name, Amen!

DAY 24

Get Out Your Feelings

*"I will bless the Lord at all times; his praise
shall continually be in my mouth."*

Psalm 34:1 NRSV

There's an infamous line that says, "You're in Your Feelings." Members of a youth organization I was volunteering for used to say this all the time—"Oh, she's in her feelings" or "Oh, he's in his feelings." The tagline is mentioned when someone gets upset, typically after some clownin' and goofin' around has taken place, and someone takes it a little too far. Then a person gets in their feelings. A person in their feelings can do a number of things—storm off, clapback, get mad or simply shut down. Our emotions sometimes get the best of us, whether we are young people playing around or adults who have stretched ourselves too thin. Let me just come right out and ask … have you gotten in your feelings with God?

How wishy-washy have you been lately? It would be the worst possibility ever to abandon Christ, simply because of our fluctuating feelings as we experience the pressures of life! Do circumstances determine your response? Do the storms of life determine your praise for the day? Is your praise dependent upon the

Faith is walking in obedience to a reality that is not yet obvious.

circumstance you're going through? Is your attitude dependent upon everything going right or how people treat and respond to you? We ought to have a mindset like David when he said, *"I will bless the Lord at ALL times: His praise shall continually be in my mouth. My soul shall make her boast in the Lord: the humble shall hear thereof, and be glad. O magnify the Lord with me, and let us exalt His name together."* (**Psalm 34:1-3 KJV**)

Faith is walking in obedience to a reality that is not yet obvious. Faith requires a continual praise and positive outlook to be offered in good and bad times—if things go your way or not! Faith is not a blank check! We don't have God as a genie to rub and get wishes. He is not waiting for us to place our orders and then give us any and everything we want. Nothing is too good for you, but it might not be good for you! It might minister to your pride instead of your humility! God wants to see if you can be trusted. If you're *faithful over a few things, He will make you ruler over many*! (**Matthew 25:21**)

So, are you in your feelings? If so, I admonish you to follow scripture which says, *"Come to me, all who are weary and burdened, and I will give you rest. Take my yoke upon you and learn from me, for I am gentle and humble in heart, and you will find rest for your souls. For my yoke is easy and my burden is light."* (**Matthew 11:28-30 NIV**) A friend of mine, Shandon, told me about her revelation of this scripture as she was talking to one of her friends, and she said it blew her mind. She said her friend had a training yoke from her grandfather's farm. The yoke was a collar and it was made to be placed around oxen to carry really heavy weights. She said the yoke had not one, but two holes: one that is for the parent oxen and one for the child. It's created in such a way that it enables the parent to take on the heavy weight to

Faith is only as good as the object in which it is placed!

take the heavy burden off of the child, but it also trains the child to learn how to carry the load on their own one day when they build up their strength!

God does the same for us. He carries all of our burdens! *"But he was wounded for our transgressions, he was bruised for our iniquities: the chastisement for our peace was upon Him; and with His stripes we are healed!"* **(Isaiah 53:5 KJV)** Jesus' burden wasn't light. He was hung on an old rugged cross just to save the same ones who cried, "Crucify Him!" Christ went through pain, agony and suffering for us—He carried our burdens so that we could learn how to carry them! There's a hymn that says take your burdens to the Lord and leave them there. Christ is carrying the burden for us.

Get out of your feelings! Faith is only as good as the object in which it is placed! Regardless of how we are feeling, our faith is not in Allah or Buddha, but in Almighty God, Jesus the Christ—who is alive and well! Faith is your response to the promises of God over your life! God says, "I will lead you." Faith responds, "I will follow." God says, "I will meet your needs." Faith responds, "It is done." Get out your feelings and walk in faith with God today!

God, I thank you for reminding me that I need to get out of my feelings. Yes, I can have and express my emotions to you, but I don't want my feelings to make me wishy-washy in my faith! Help me today to maintain not only a positive attitude, but to really cast my cares, my burdens and my struggles over to you! Lord, I ask that you carry my weight today! I ask that you would pick up the slack for me today where I fall short. Help me to have a praise on my lips regardless of what the day may bring! I give you glory Lord, for it all belongs to you. In Jesus name, Amen!

What I Took From Today's Devotional Is:

_____

_____

_____

_____

I Realize I Still Struggle and Will Work On:

_____

_____

_____

_____

I Will Cast Out These Negative Thoughts, Fears, and Insecurities Today:

_____

_____

_____

_____

I Will Speak These Positive Affirmations Over Myself Today:

_____

_____

_____

_____

I will have a good day and it will be better than yesterday!
In Jesus Name, Amen!

DAY 25

Divine Assurance

"...Let us draw near to God with a sincere heart and with the full assurance that faith brings, having our hearts sprinkled to cleanse us from a guilty conscience and having our bodies washed with pure water."

Hebrews 10:22 NIV

There are so many different types of insurances. If you own a car, you know we have to have car insurance to drive. If you have a house, you know there is homeowner's insurance that you have to purchase. Not to mention, the various kinds of life insurance policies that are available as well. There are so many different carriers and companies that you can choose from for your car, house and life insurance policies. We buy these products not only because we have to, but because if anything goes wrong, we can fall back on that policy to help cover the cost of any damages or replacements. We buy life insurance to cover burial expenses and maybe even leave something for our loved ones. The point is, it's our fallback plan. We rely on our policies to be there for us when we need them. If we didn't have them, we would be on our own—it would be up to us to figure out. When I thought about the insurance(s) we purchase and the payment(s) that come

Assurance is resting in the promises of God.

around like clock-work, it dawned on me that we not only have to live with insurance, but we need to live in assurance!

Assurance, as defined by the Easton's Bible dictionary is, "The pledge God has given that His revelation is true and worthy of acceptance." The Merriam-Webster dictionary defines assurance as, "Being certain in the mind...confidence of mind or manner; excessive self-confidence." It is written in **Hebrews 10:22 NIV**, "*...let us draw near to God with a sincere heart and with the full assurance that faith brings, having our hearts sprinkled to cleanse us from a guilty conscience and having our bodies washed with pure water.*" The writer of **Colossians 2:2-3 NIV** says, "*My goal is that they may be encouraged in heart and united in love, so that they may have the full riches of complete understanding, in order that they may know the mystery of God, namely, Christ, in whom all the treasures of wisdom and knowledge.*" We ought to have a fullness of faith in God that leaves no room for doubt.

Assurance has a certain conviction, something that is un-wavered and can't be moved. It is written in **Hebrews 6:11-12 NIV**, "*We want each of you to show this same diligence to the very end, so that what you hope for may be fully realized. We do not want you to become lazy, but to imitate those who through faith and patience inherit what has been promised.*" Assurance is resting in the promises of God. There's a song that my grandma used to sing. She liked the second verse of the hymn that said, "Standing on the promises that cannot fail. When the howling storms of doubt and fear assail. By the living Word of God I shall prevail, standing on the promises of God. Standing, standing, standing on the promises of God my Savior. Standing, standing, I'm standing on the promises of God." That's our assurance!

In the midst of a chaotic world and havoc breaking out all

around us, assurance of a person's security in God is crucial. This assurance is not based on abilities, human resources, conditions, networks, connections or inventiveness, but it is based on confidence and power of Almighty God to care for His children. Assurance in God provides an anchor of confidence and hope despite the presence of frustration or pain! The writer of **Hebrews 6:18 NIV** says, *"God did this so that, by two unchangeable things in which it is impossible for God to lie, we who have fled to take hold of the hope set before us may be greatly encouraged."* God is our refuge and He can always be counted on!

> ## Assurance is not the result of faith, it is the true essence of faith.

Assurance is not the result of faith, it is the true essence of faith. There's a hymn that says, "Blessed assurance, Jesus is mine. Oh what a foretaste of glory divine. Heir of salvation, purchase of God. Born of His Spirit, washed in His blood. This is my story, this is my song. Praising my Savior all the day long. This is my story, this is my song. Praising my Savior all the day long." We have assurance in God. Don't just rely on your insurance; but rely on the assurance of Christ our King.

Lord, thank you for divine assurance today. I know that you are with me and I put my trust in you. Just as I count on my insurance to be there for me, I know you are there for me and that is my assurance! I stand on your Word. I stand on your promises. I believe that you are my protection, you are my covering and you will not only provide for me, but you will also guide me! Thank you God, for giving me my true life's assurance today and helping me to walk in it. In Jesus name, Amen.

What I Took From Today's Devotional Is:

_____

_____

_____

_____

I Realize I Still Struggle and Will Work On:

_____

_____

_____

_____

I Will Cast Out These Negative Thoughts, Fears, and Insecurities Today:

_____

_____

_____

_____

I Will Speak These Positive Affirmations Over Myself Today:

_____

_____

_____

_____

I will have a good day and it will be better than yesterday!
In Jesus Name, Amen!

DAY 26

Get Out of Your Own Way

*"Trust in the Lord with all your heart, and lean
not on your own understanding; in all your ways
acknowledge Him, and He shall direct your paths!"*
Proverbs 3:5-6 NKJV

If you're like me, at times, God can't help me because I'm in the way. I can be in my own way whether it's due to self-doubt, second-guessing, my constant planning, my own motives and agenda, or even fear. I get in my own way. Maybe that is you today. What is it that God wants to do in your life? Have you conjured and devised your own plan to "help" God out? Have you intervened prematurely? Maybe you've heard the word of the Lord and were waiting for instructions, but then decided to go ahead and find your own path? Are you in your own way???

This reminds me of the story of Abraham and Sarah. In **Genesis 15**, the word of the Lord came to Abram declaring that he would have an heir. In **Genesis 16**, Sarai went to Abram and said the Lord restrained her from having children, so she suggested that he sleep her maid-servant Hagar. He could have a son that way. Sarai wanted to help God out with the word HE had given her. Isn't that funny?! She decided to take actions into her own hands to fulfill the promise her own way. Abram and

Hagar conceived a son, Ishmael. Sarai then gets mad and treats Hagar badly and as a result, Hagar flees. The Lord appears to Hagar, tells her to go back to Sarai and makes a promise to her and her family. Despite Abram and Sarai's disobedience, God had to come back in **Genesis 17** to reconfirm the word He spoke to them. He changed their names (Abram to Abraham and Sarai to Sarah), prophesied Isaac's birth, and declared he would take care of Ishmael.

The purpose of mentioning this occurrence in the Bible is to call out how getting in the way interrupts the move of God in our lives! Sarah didn't believe the word of the Lord because her present condition forced her to believe her reality and not what God said. This occurs so often in our own lives—we hear what God said, but it's hard to believe it when we can only see one side, one perspective of our human condition. We often believe what our present reality says over God's word for our lives. Sarah knew she was old and didn't see how conceiving a child would happen, so she took matters into her own hands. This caused more issues and more drama. She resented the other woman and got mad because of Ishmael—but it was her idea! Isn't that just like us—to see our weaknesses and inabilities, count ourselves out, devise plans and schemes to make things work, and end up digging ourselves into a deeper hole that God then has to get us out of.

> God is not controlled by anything or anyone outside of Himself!

How many of us received a word from the Lord or have prayed on some things but then went ahead and initiated on God's behalf? Just because the Lord spoke it doesn't mean He needs <u>you</u> to work it out for Him. God is not controlled by anything or anyone outside of Himself! He's got this! The writer of **Isaiah 46:11 KJV** says, *"...I have spoken it, I will* *also bring it to pass; I have purposed it, I will also do it."* The only help He needs from you is for you trust in Him, trust in what He said and wait for the manifestation of the Lord. We must not get in the way! If we get in the way, we get in our own way! We have to do as the scripture says in **Proverbs 3:5-6 KJV**, *"Trust in the Lord with all thine heart; and lean not unto thine own understanding. In all thy ways acknowledge Him, and He shall direct thy paths!"* So, what do you do while you wait? In the interim, between what God said and seeing it come to fruition, while you're waiting on the manifestation to happen—don't stop praising, don't stop praying and don't stop preparing!

Praise—Praise God for the word you received! Thank God for simply speaking! Thank God for the promise that He has provided over your life! Thank God for the idea. Praise God for the vision. Praise God for the new outlook on life! Praise God for His Word, which never comes back void! *"So shall My word be that goes out from my mouth; it shall not return to me empty, but it shall accomplish that which I purpose, and succeed in the thing for which I sent it."* **(Isaiah 55:11 NRSV)**

Pray—Seek the Lord to guide you in what you need to do! Maybe He is telling you to act, make moves, do research. Maybe He is telling you be to be still and rest while you wait! Your instructions are dependent on you hearing from the Lord. Seek His instructions and not your emotions. Seek His way and not your own. Seek His advice and not your friends! *"Ask, and it will be given you; search, and you will find; knock, and the door will be opened for you. For everyone who asks receives, and everyone who searches finds, and for everyone who knocks, the door will be opened."* **(Matthew 7:7-8 NRSV)** *"Do not be anxious about anything, but in every situation, by prayer and petition, with thanksgiving, present your request to God."*

(Philippians 4:6-7 NIV) *"This is the confidence we have in approaching God: that if we ask anything according to His will, He hears us."* **(1 John 5:14 NIV)**

Prepare—Prepare yourself for what you believe is about to happen! Maybe the Lord is telling you to budget and save money or invest. Maybe the Lord needs you to read more, not only your Word, but other industry books. Maybe the Lord is telling you to seek a mentor who has gone down the road you are about to travel. Maybe the Lord wants you to seek counseling. Whatever it is that will help you discern and grow in your wisdom, you have to prepare yourself for the blessing you are believing God for! A farmer prepares for a harvest by planting his crops. A mother prepares for a new baby by storing diapers and clothes in a nursery. As children of God, we have to prepare ourselves physically, financially, mentally, emotionally and spiritually for the manifestation of the blessing that is on the way! *"Prepare yourself and be ready, you and all your companies that are gathered about you; and be a guard for them."* **(Ezekiel 38:7 NKJV)** *"For we are His* Get out *workmanship, created in Christ Jesus for good works,* of your *which God prepared beforehand so that we would* own way! *walk in them."* **(Ephesians 2:10 NKJV)** *"Therefore, prepare your minds for action; discipline yourselves; set all your hope on grace that Jesus Christ will bring you when he is revealed."* **(1 Peter 1:13 NRSV)**

So, get out of your own way! Allow the Lord to be your guide and wait patiently for the manifestation of God's Word! And while you wait, praise, pray and prepare.

Lord, thank you for the Word you have spoken over my life! I praise you for not giving up on me in spite of my disobedience! Help me to trust you wholeheartedly, to depend on you, and to allow the Word you have spoken to come to pass. Help me to not get in my own way. Help me to not get in your way. I need you to guide and instruct me in the way I should go! And Lord, while I wait on the manifestation to come, I will praise you, I will pray and I will prepare! In Jesus name, Amen.

What I Took From Today's Devotional Is:

_____

_____

_____

_____

I Realize I Still Struggle and Will Work On:

_____

_____

_____

_____

I Will Cast Out These Negative Thoughts, Fears, and Insecurities Today:

_____

_____

_____

_____

I Will Speak These Positive Affirmations Over Myself Today:

_____

_____

_____

_____

I will have a good day and it will be better than yesterday!
In Jesus Name, Amen!

DAY 27

B.L.I.N.D.—Bound Looking In Narrow Directions

"Jesus said to him, 'Stand up, take your mat and walk."
John 5:8 NRSV

Too many times have we allowed ourselves to settle for less than what we deserve. This goes for men and women! I'm not talking about not being content, I'm talking about when you know you deserve better, but you just don't do better. For whatever reason, we hang on to a bad relationship, business partnership, career—you name it, using excuses as to why we stay put. We limit ourselves by being **B.L.I.N.D.—Bound Looking In Narrow Directions.** If the narrow way is all you see, then you aren't expanding your view and mindset to something more that's out there. When we do this, we limit our mind, our abilities and our progress to achieve all that God would have for us. By remaining stagnant, we never get to see what is beyond our current viewpoint.

> We limit ourselves by being **B.L.I.N.D.— Bound Looking In Narrow Directions.**

Ok, so I may need to give you some examples to bring my point across. How many times have you gone back to your hometown and have seen the same people sitting on the same corners, wearing the same varsity jacket from high school? And all they talk about is the good ole days? Nothing is wrong with reminiscing, but the problem occurs when you live there. Someone can live so far in the past and what was, that they aren't present in what is and what can be! That's **B.L.I.N.D.!** I know of people who have never ventured outside of the 50-mile radius of their city. Hanging around the same people, going to the same places and hangouts, with the same routine every weekend. They have no desire to even visit another state, let alone try and go outside of the country. Now, I get the concerns of traveling. I also understand loving your friends and having favorite spots to go to. There is nothing wrong with that; but when your mind is so conditioned to never expand your horizons, that's living **B.L.I.N.D.—B**ound **L**ooking **I**n **N**arrow **D**irections.

> Someone can live so far in the past and what was, that they aren't present in what is and what can be!

Let me try to explain it a different way. What about those friends you have who never have anything positive to say about someone else? You can always count on that one person to gossip about someone whether their attire, shoes, hair, the way they walk, talk—Nothing is ever positive! That person limits their view of people. It really shows how small minded they really are. In the words of Eleanor Roosevelt, *"Great minds discuss ideas; average minds discuss events; small minds discuss people."* People who gossip are living **B.L.I.N.D.—B**ound **L**ooking **I**n **N**arrow **D**irections. What about others who make every excuse in the book as to why they can't do something. They either start something and never finish or they are constantly complaining. It's always someone else's fault. They point the blame at someone or something, and never take responsibility or ownership for their own actions. Yes, things happen and sometimes we are dealt a bad hand, but what we do with that hand and the effort we put forward to play with what we have is key! That person is limited and is living **B.L.I.N.D.—B**ound **L**ooking **I**n **N**arrow **D**irections.

In **John 5 NRSV**, there is a man who did the same thing. He was a paralytic who had been sick for over 38 years! Jesus saw him lying there and knew he had been there a long time. He asks the man, *"Do you want to be made well?"* (v.6) Now, any of us reading this, we would think that the next reply from the man's mouth would have been something like, "Uhm duh, absolutely, no question, YES I DO!" But none of that comes out of his mouth. The man doesn't respond with what he actually wants to have occur and what he has been waiting so long for. Instead he provides an excuse to explain his circumstances. He replies with, *"Sir, I have no one to put me in the pool when the water is stirred up; and while I am making my way, someone else steps down ahead of me."* (v.7) Jesus simply responds with, *"Stand up, take your mat and walk."* (v.8) The rest of the scripture says, *"At once, the man was made well, and he took up his mat and began to walk."* (v.9) Here's what's amazing to me: despite his excuse and limitations, Jesus didn't leave him where he was! Jesus didn't leave him the way He found him. Jesus healed him anyway! Despite our own limitations and excuses, Jesus will never leave us where we are! God is not confined to our preconceived notions, nor our **B.L.I.N.D.** way of living. He will grant us wholeness, healing and restoration just like he did for this man!

The issue with this text is not only the excuse the man had, but the response from the people, the Jews. See, Jesus was their enemy because He threatened their power, authority and their very perception of reality. The Sabbath law was used as their defense. The Jews focused on challenging Jesus and the conventional order, whereas Jesus focused on the healed man and the man's new life, which brought about new possibilities. The objection to Jesus healing the man in this encounter, is really a rejection of the possibility of new and unprecedented ways of knowing God! I'm so glad God is not confined to our structure or rules!

God wants us to experience new life today! We can experience new perspectives of living and new ways of ordering our lives the way Christ intends! You don't have to live **B.L.I.N.D.—** **B**ound **L**ooking **I**n **N**arrow **D**irections. Don't live with narrow thinking and narrow mindsets. Be free to live in the new possibilities that are real for you today through Christ! There's a song my dad used to always sing, and the lyrics are, "I am free. Praise the Lord I'm free. No longer bound. No more chains holding me. My soul is resting, it's such a blessing. Praise the Lord, Hallelujah I'm free!" Be free today! You are free to live the unrestricted, unstructured and unconfined life you were meant to live!

> *Lord, thank you for letting me see the areas where I am B.L.I.N.D. in my life. Lord, I don't want to be bound looking and living in narrow directions. I want to live freely and I need you to broaden my horizon. Broaden my thinking Lord! Clear my mind so I can see the possibilities that are available to me. Allow my family to experience a freedom, Lord that takes off all restrictions and bondage. I believe that I will live a life that is no longer B.L.I.N.D. and no longer bound. In Jesus name, Amen!*

What I Took From Today's Devotional Is:

_____

_____

_____

_____

I Realize I Still Struggle and Will Work On:

_____

_____

_____

_____

I Will Cast Out These Negative Thoughts, Fears, and Insecurities Today:

_____

_____

_____

_____

I Will Speak These Positive Affirmations Over Myself Today:

_____

_____

_____

_____

I will have a good day and it will be better than yesterday!
In Jesus Name, Amen!

DAY 28

It's On The Way

"But they that wait upon the Lord shall renew their strength; they shall mount up with wings as eagles; they shall run, and not be weary; they shall walk, and not faint."

Isaiah 40:31 KJV

Something about me that many people know is that I love plays! I love to go to all kinds of shows, whether ballet or opera, musicals, or my all-time favorite Broadway shows! I saw the Lion King LIVE in New York City and absolutely fell in love! Lion King is #1 on my list! Recently, I was supposed to see *Hamilton* when it came to Dallas, but the only night that wasn't sold out was the night I had to present in class. Needless to say, I was extremely upset about not being able to attend what I felt was a once in a lifetime opportunity! (Ok, I digress).

During these shows though, it is inevitable that a climax or a pivotal point will occur right before the curtains will close. The lights will come on and the announcer will say something to the extent of, *"We will now have a short 15 minute intermission."* Intermission is the part in-between scenes of a play or show that allows you to reprieve for a moment, gather yourself, use the restroom and then head back in to finish the rest of the show. It heightens the suspense and leaves you wondering how things will turn out in the end. When the intermission is about to be over, the lights will flicker and then finally dim to black. The curtains will reopen to continue with the rest of the show.

Now, what does this have to do with today's devotional title? There is always an intermission, the infamous waiting period, between what just happened and the next phase. Every one of us has experienced a waiting period, an intermission, like that. Maybe you are in one right now! During that intermission and brief stint of waiting for the revelation and manifestation to occur, we have to know that IT'S ON THE WAY! The intermission is a period to not only allow God to intervene and finish the story, but to ultimately produce something within us while we wait!

The Bible is full of so many people who had an intermission, the period between their wait and their "It's On The Way!"

- In the book of **Daniel**, Daniel is thrown into the lions' den because of his continued prayers to His God despite orders from the king. Even when he is thrown into the lions' den, Daniel's response was to pray and fast; to trust in the salvation of the Lord. Daniel was not touched by any of the lions in that den. We have a responsibility in our waiting, to continue to obey, trust and seek God, and believe our deliverance is on the way!

- In the Gospels (**Matthew 9, Mark 5, and Luke 8**), we find a woman with an issue of blood. She has been bleeding for 12 long years! We don't know how she came to be this way, but what we do know is that she was considered "unclean" and anything she touched was deemed to be "unclean." She waited for a cure, sought everything possible, and she waited. Then she heard of Jesus coming to town. She pressed her way through the crowd and touched the hem of His garment!

Immediately, she was healed! In our waiting, we have to be persistent and know healing is on the way!

- In the book of **Esther**, we find that once she becomes queen, she learns of Haman's plot to kill the Jews. Her cousin, Mordecai had an issue because he refused to bow down to Haman. As a result, Haman not only wanted to kill Mordecai, but eradicate all of his people. Esther, despite not being able to approach the king without being summoned, makes up in her mind, *"If I perish, I perish."* (**Esther 4:16**) One woman's commitment and bravery saves her people! We have to know that it is on the way because God is working behind the scenes, orchestrating things together, to bring about His divine purpose!

During your intermission, between your waiting and "It's On the Way," ask yourself:

- What is God trying to show me or tell me?
- What is God trying to instill in me during this time? Is it meant to build my character, increase my stamina, develop patience, increase my trust in Him?

It's been said that patience is a virtue! It's so true. To explain virtue, I will use the dictionary's definition that says, *"Virtue is moral excellence, conformity of one's life and conduct."* The Fruit of the Spirit describes these virtues—biblical attributes that we should all live by: love, joy, peace, patience (longsuffering), kindness, goodness, faithfulness, gentleness and self-control. (**Galatians 5:22-23**) Our intermission may be instilling in us a deeper sense of these

But trust and believe It's On The Way!

biblical attributes that the Lord wants to have exude from our lives!

There are so many possibilities as to why God may have you in "intermission," but trust and believe It's On The Way! Your spirit has to be reaffirmed that your miracle is on the way! Your breakthrough is on the way! Your hope is being restored because it's on the way! This is not a prosperity word, but a fact that must be realized, internalized and believed! Scripture says, *"But they that wait upon the Lord shall renew their strength; they shall mount up with wings as eagles; they shall run, and not be weary; and they shall walk, and not faint."* (**Isaiah 40:31 KJV**) In our intermission, our waiting, Christ renews, changes, challenges and strengthens us! The psalmist says in **Psalm 27:14 KJV,** *"Wait on the Lord: be of good courage, and He shall strengthen thine heart: wait, I say, on the Lord!"*

In our intermission, our waiting, Christ renews, changes, challenges and strengthens us!

You may be waiting for justice, healing, a marriage restored, financial breakthrough, relationships mended, forgiveness, loved ones to be saved, children to come back home, answers and guidance, but in your waiting, believe today—It's On The Way!

Lord, thank you for the confirmation today that my miracle is on the way! Thank you for confirming that my intermission, my waiting period, is strengthening me for what's to come! Lord, I put my trust in you while I wait. Help me to not get weary, but to know that you are working things out on the backend. I know you are orchestrating a miracle in my life! Help me to be strong, to seek you while I wait, and to believe that it's on the way! In Jesus name, Amen!

What I Took From Today's Devotional Is:

_____

_____

_____

_____

I Realize I Still Struggle and Will Work On:

_____

_____

_____

_____

I Will Cast Out These Negative Thoughts, Fears, and Insecurities Today:

_____

_____

_____

_____

I Will Speak These Positive Affirmations Over Myself Today:

_____

_____

_____

_____

I will have a good day and it will be better than yesterday!
In Jesus Name, Amen!

DAY 29
Triumph

"But thanks be to God, who in Christ always leads us in triumphal procession, and through us spreads in every place the fragrance that comes from knowing Him."
2 Corinthians 2:14 NRSV

We have victory in Christ! Even when it looks like we will be defeated; when it looks like our backs are against the wall; when it looks like all hope is gone—you can be assured you have victory! We have victory in and through Christ! You have victory because the writer of **Philippians 4:13 KJV** says, *"I can do all things through Christ which strengtheneth me."* You have to know today that you walk in victory! Tye Tribbett & G.A. has a song called Victory and the lyrics say, *"I thought I lost, but actually I won. For by His blood we all have overcome. There is no failure, our God can never lose. And that same power it now belongs to you. Now it's time to celebrate, all banners raised. I got the victory, the victory. Because the devil is defeated and God be praised. I got the victory, the victory. Every situation I face I win. I got the victory, the victory. And everything works for my good in the end. I got the victory, the victory."* I like this part of the song because it continues and says, *"Somebody who's listening, right now you think you're losing. You feel like you can't win, cause you've tried everything. Greater is He that is within you, don't*

doubt, whatever you're in now, God said, you have to come out."
You can't give up! You can't quit! This is not the time to
throw in the towel! You have the victory and there's victory in
Jesus!

Here's what's interesting: I thought victory and living
victorious was as good as it could get, but I was wrong! There is
still a level higher and that is triumph! We can live triumphantly!
Let me explain. In **2 Kings 5**, the unnamed Aramean king
repeatedly devised secret plans to attack Israel, but each time the
prophet Elisha learned of the plans through His God-given gifts.
He would then pass the secrets on to the Israelites who would
use the information to prevent the king from accomplishing
what he intended. In chapter 6, they singled out the prophet
Elisha, finding out that he was the cause for the leaks and
their plans not succeeding. As a result, the king sent an entire
army—horses and chariots of fire, to
capture Elisha.

Elisha's attendant wakes up one
morning and he is astonished by all of
the troops that he saw. His attendant
was terrified! Elisha looks out and
sees the army with chariots of fire

> God will not only
> make you victorious,
> but He will cause
> your life to be lived
> triumphantly!

surrounding him, and his response was to pray! The prophet
prays to God. He asks God to strike the army blind. Though
they aren't completely blind, Elisha is able to send them in the
wrong direction. Isn't it funny that when the enemy devises
a plan to scheme and capture, there's always a way of escape
that is made! The prophet Elisha, whom the great army was
sent to capture, tells them that they are going in the wrong
direction. When he volunteers to lead them to the man they
seek to capture, they blindly follow him. Elisha then brings
them to Samaria, where the Israelites had military superiority.

He then prays for their sight to be restored and they realize where they are.

Here is what is remarkable! Instead of invoking violence on them and killing them, Elisha tells the king to extend hospitality to the enemy troops and to release them. I guess there is nothing more humiliating than for the great invading army to be fed and then sent on their way. As a result, they no longer harassed Israel.

This epic encounter is one of not only victory, but of triumph! Elisha, in the midst of chaos and trouble surrounding him, doesn't freak out, run in fear, or anything. We see him stand his ground and pray. The victory is that no harm comes to Elisha. But God does one even better! When the opportunity presents itself for revenge, there is no retaliation! Elisha encourages the Israelites to welcome the enemy army in, to feed them, and then send them on their way. The king and the army never bothered them again. THAT IS TRIUMPH! What the enemy meant for evil, God will turn it around for good! It is written in **Genesis 50:20 KJV**, *"But as for you, ye thought evil against me; but God meant it unto good, to bring it to pass, as it is this day, to save much people alive."*

Walk in victory and live in triumph!

Even if you are up against what feels like a massive army and the weight of the world is on you, take heart because God is with you! God will not only make you victorious, but He will cause your life to be lived triumphantly! The writer of **2 Corinthians 2:14 NRSV** says, *"But thanks be to God, who in Christ always leads in triumphal procession, and through us spreads in every place the fragrance that comes from knowing him."* Walk in victory and live in triumph!

Lord, thank you for letting me know that when the world seems to come against me, I can trust in you. God, you never lose. Help me today to walk not only in victory, but to walk in triumph. Your Word covers, your Spirit protects, and you have all power in your hands! Lord, thank you for reminding me that I can do all things through Christ who strengthens me. In Jesus name, Amen!

What I Took From Today's Devotional Is:

_____

_____

_____

_____

I Realize I Still Struggle and Will Work On:

_____

_____

_____

_____

I Will Cast Out These Negative Thoughts, Fears, and Insecurities Today:

_____

_____

_____

_____

I Will Speak These Positive Affirmations Over Myself Today:

_____

_____

_____

_____

I will have a good day and it will be better than yesterday!
In Jesus Name, Amen!

DAY 30

New Season

*"For everything there is a season, and a time
for every matter under heaven."*

Ecclesiastes 3:1 NRSV

Seasons come and seasons go, but with each season comes something new and refreshing. Summer comes with the heat of the sun and the excitement to be free and relaxed on vacation. The coolness of fall brings the crisp, gentle breeze that causes colorful leaves to fall to the ground. The peaceful, calm and glittering snow that comes with winter and the holidays that brings everyone together again to share the joys and memories of loved ones. The renewing spring comes with trees and flowers that bud again and birds that begin to fill the air as they chirp in the wind.

Some don't like the snow and cold of winter. They don't like scraping off car windows and salting the sidewalks, but there is something about the holidays during the winter season. Bringing family together and reminiscing about good times make it all worthwhile. Some don't like summer's brutal heat. They hate to be outside sweating. They would prefer to stay in the house with the air conditioning. But, summer has exciting times of cookouts,

Life is a journey not a destination!

vacations and fun. Each season has its waves of good and bad, pros and cons.

Restoration is sometimes brought about by the constant cycle of death and rebirth. This is life. Life is a journey not a destination! It is filled with ups and downs, good and bad, life and death. But life is meant to be lived! The key is to learn something in each season. My dad once told me, "You have to learn your rhythm. Just like music has its own beat, you have your own rhythm that your life moves to. Just like seasons change; when one cycle ends a new cycle begins, you have to learn your cycle." So, what's your rhythm? What is your life's beat? What's your cycle? The writer of **Ecclesiastes 3:1 NRSV** says, *"For everything there is a season, and a time for every matter under heaven..."* We don't operate in our time, but in God's time. He is the eternal timekeeper! Don't get discouraged with life and where you are. Don't get down on yourself and upset at the frustrating moments and bad times of life. Know there will be an upswing coming soon! You might be on the downbeat right now, but the upbeat is coming! *"...Weeping may endure for a night, but joy cometh in the morning."* (**Psalm 30:5 KJV**) The writer of **Isaiah 43:19 NRSV** says, *"I am about to do a new thing; now it springs forth, do you not perceive it? I will make a way in the wilderness and rivers in the desert."* The writer of **2 Corinthians 5:16 NKJV** says, *"Therefore, if anyone is in Christ, he is a new creation; old things have passed away; behold, all things have become new."*

No matter where you are in life, you can make a new start today! You don't have to wait until nature actually changes seasons, and you don't have to wait for a new year to start a new resolution! Make up in your mind that

Make up in your mind that your new season starts now!

your new season starts now! Live to a new beat! Live to a new rhythm! You can't change the past. You can't do anything about yesterday because it's already gone, it already happened—but you can do something about your today and prepare for your tomorrow!

So, what are you waiting for? Your new season is now—lift up your foot and start moving!

God, I thank you that my new season starts now! I thank you that today I am changing my perspective on life and am going to learn from the cycles and seasons I've been in. I believe that I am walking in a new purpose and I am going to strive for greater things that are up ahead. My time is not up, but starts now! In Jesus name, Amen.

What I Took From Today's Devotional Is:

_____

_____

_____

_____

I Realize I Still Struggle and Will Work On:

_____

_____

_____

_____

I Will Cast Out These Negative Thoughts, Fears, and Insecurities Today:

_____

_____

_____

_____

I Will Speak These Positive Affirmations Over Myself Today:

_____

_____

_____

_____

I will have a good day and it will be better than yesterday!
In Jesus Name, Amen!

To Every Reader:
Better days are ahead!

Your latter will be greater than your past!

Haggai 2:9 NIV
"The glory of this present house will be greater than the glory of the former house,' says the Lord Almighty. 'And in this place I will grant peace,' declares the Lord Almighty."

1 Corinthians 2:9 NIV
"...What no eye has seen, what no ear has heard, and what no human mind has conceived"—the things God has prepared for those who love Him."

God's Richest Blessings Be Upon You!

ABOUT THE AUTHOR

Rev. Nerissa Elaine Grigsby

NERISSA GRIGSBY is a multi-faceted and well-rounded individual with many passions! She was licensed to preach the gospel on December 19, 2003. She served as the Youth and Young Adult Pastor of Central Baptist Church in Pittsburgh, PA, where her father, Rev. Victor J. Grigsby is the Pastor. She served as the Youth & Young Adult Pastor until 2010 and on December 5, 2010, she completed her catechism and was ordained. She was then appointed as the Associate Pastor of Worship, where she served 11 different ministries. During this time, Rev. Grigsby received her Bachelor of Arts degree from California University of PA (2007) and a Master of Arts degree from Point Park University (2009).

Very adamant about serving in ministry and simultaneously climbing the corporate ladder, Rev. Grigsby accepted a corporate position and moved to St. Louis, MO in 2011. She continued to be involved in ministry and she even branched into entrepreneurship. She began a mentoring program for girls ages 13-17. She also created a seminar and pageant to empower young girls and help cultivate them personally and spiritually.

In 2015, Rev. Grigsby accepted her company's request to

relocate to Dallas, TX where she currently resides. She is a member of Friendship West Baptist Church, where Rev. Dr. Frederick Douglas Haynes III is the Pastor.

In 2020, Rev. Grigsby received her Master of Divinity (MDiv) degree and graduated Magna Cum Laude, from Southern Methodist University (SMU) Perkins School of Theology. She is currently enrolled at SMU, pursuing her Doctorate of Ministry (DMin) Degree and anticipates graduating in 2023.

She pursues her passions, serving as the Founder and CEO of Real Unstructured, nonprofit organization; which is an educational platform to provide spiritual, personal and professional development skills. It is also a platform designed for millennials to showcase their God-given gifts and talents with the world, who have used unstructured, unconventional and unapologetic means to pursue their dreams. These young people have followed their passions and now their gifts and talents are working for them! Rev. Grigsby not only spotlights these young people, but she also provides inspirational words of encouragement to help others go after their dreams and step out on faith with the gifts and talents that God has given them! Rev. Grigsby also meets with marketplace leaders to gain insight and knowledge to ensure millennials are staying on the cusp of industry standards and topics.

She is also the Founder and CEO of Grigsby Nine Legacy (GNL) Consulting LLC, which is a consulting agency where companies and organizations can solicit for speaking engagements, project and risk management sessions, as well as facilitation for professional training and seminars.

Rev. Grigsby loves God and has a heart for lost souls. She speaks to every generation, with Jesus' message of hope, empowerment, and love. She desires for every unbeliever to be saved and for believers in Christ to possess their God-given purpose, and become effective in the Kingdom of God! Her assignment in the Kingdom is to do what the Lord told her:

The word of the LORD came to her, saying, *"Before I formed you in the womb I knew you, before you were born I set you apart; I appointed you as a prophet to the nations." Then the LORD reached out his hand and touched my mouth and said to me, "I have put my words in your mouth. See, today I appoint you over nations and kingdoms to uproot and tear down, to destroy and overthrow, to build and to plant."* (**Jeremiah 1:4-5, 9-10 NIV**)